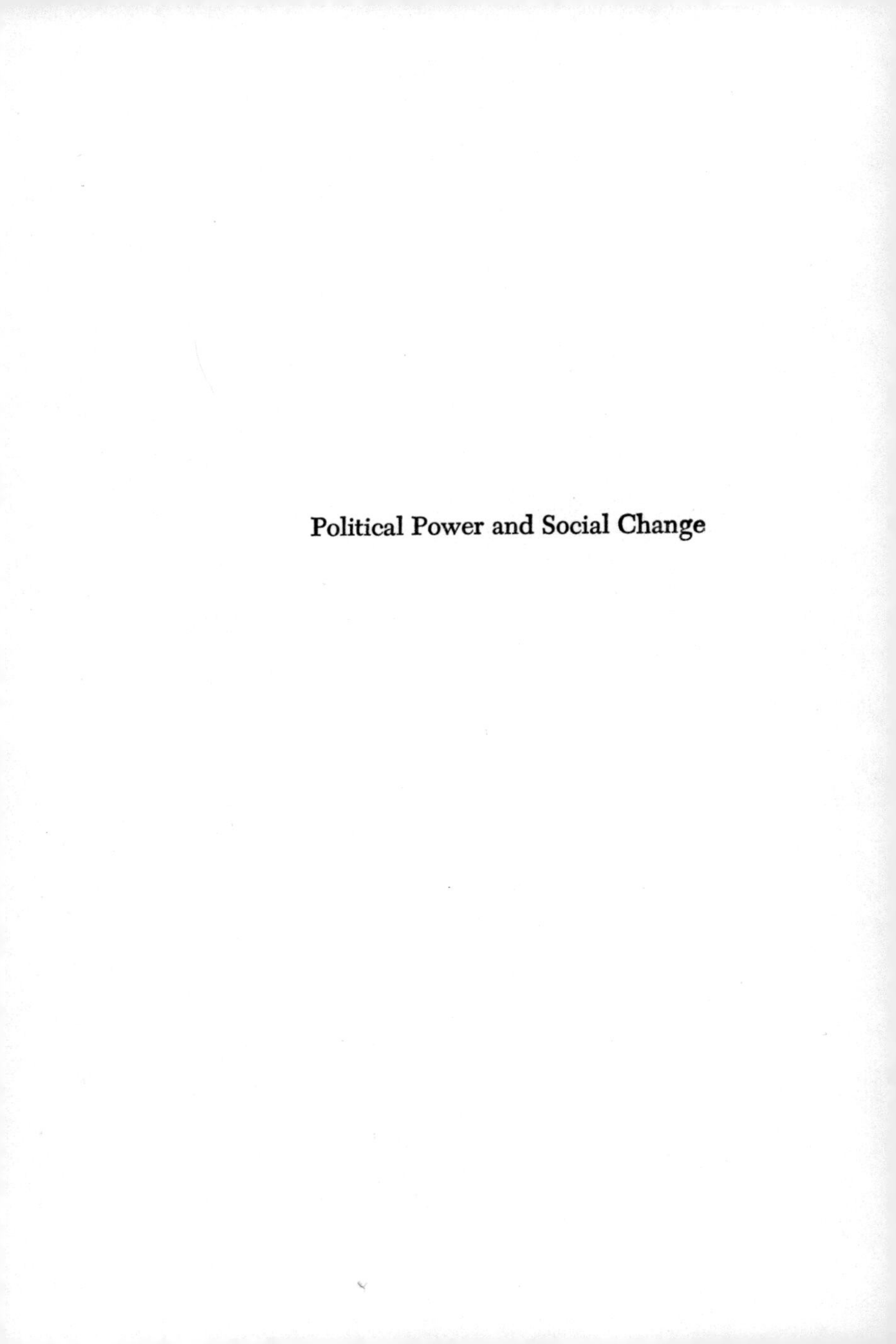

Political Power and Social Change

Peter H. Odegard

Political Power & Social Change

Rutgers University Press
New Brunswick, New Jersey

Library of Congress Catalogue Card Number: 65–28215

Grateful acknowledgment is made for permission to quote the following material:

Harcourt, Brace & World, Inc., for T. S. Eliot's "Little Gidding" in "The Four Quartets," *Complete Poems and Plays* (New York, 1952).

Little, Brown & Company for Ogden Nash's "The Miraculous Countdown" in *Everyone but Thee and Me* (Copyright 1962 by Ogden Nash).

Dodd, Mead & Company, Thomas Y. Crowell Company, and A. & C. Black, Ltd., for W. H. Mallock's translation of "No Single Thing Abides" by Titus Lucretius Carus.

Contents

The 1965 Brown and Haley Lectures are the thirteenth of a series that has been given annually at the University of Puget Sound, Tacoma, Washington, by a scholar distinguished for his work in the Social Studies or the Humanities. The purpose of these lectures is to present original analyses of some intellectual problems confronting the present age.

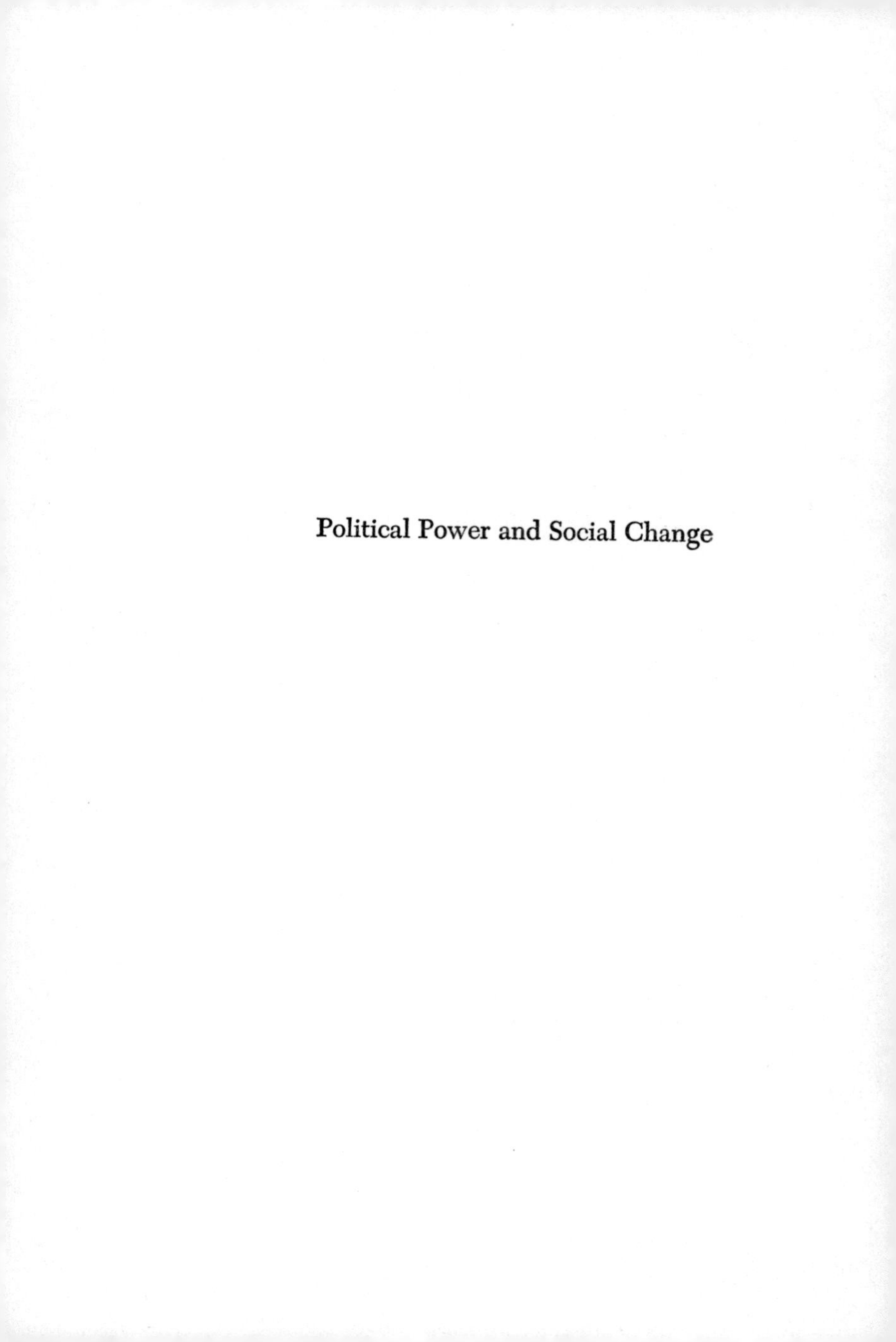

Political Power and Social Change

I

"No single thing abides"

Heraclitus (of Ephesus), six centuries before Christ, observed that nothing in the universe is constant —or, if you prefer, that the only constant thing is change itself.

Nor was this idea original with him. From the beginning of human life on this planet, man has been obsessed with a search for security in a universe of continuous and constant change. Said Lucretius:

No single thing abides; but all things flow.
Fragment to fragment clings—the things thus grow
Until we know and name them. By degrees
They melt, and are no more the things we know.

Globed from the atoms falling slow or swift
I see the suns, I see the systems lift
Their forms; but even the systems and the suns
*Shall go back slowly to the eternal drift.**

Permanence and change

In this universe of everlasting and ceaseless change, the human mind looks for signs of law and order to give it some measure of stability and permanence. In the recurrent rising and setting of the sun, the orderly and predictable cycle of the seasons, of life and death among men and animals, plants and planets, in all this we find reason to believe that law and order are attributes even of the physical universe about us. We even profess to find evidence of immutable and everlasting laws of nature to govern in the affairs of men. In the monuments of ancient cultures, in the cycle of civilizations that Spengler, Toynbee, and others have described, and in the continuity of human history

* "No Single Thing Abides" by Titus Lucretius Carus, translated by W. H. Mallock, from *Imagination's Other Place*, compiled by Helen Plotz (New York: Thomas Y. Crowell, 1955), p. 9.

itself, we look for signs to confirm our faith in these laws of nature and of nature's God.

Knowing, or at any rate believing, that the ceaseless changes which occur in the physical universe and in our human condition occur in an orderly fashion according to immutable laws, we are comforted in the thought that the more things change the more they remain the same.

Thus through the ages we have grown accustomed to change, believing with Ecclesiastes that

> One generation passeth away, and another generation cometh: but the earth abideth forever.

Unhappily this notion of smooth and orderly transition from one generation to another or from one culture or civilization to another in a world that "abideth forever" has been rudely challenged. It has been challenged by the knowledge that cultural changes, like changes in living organisms, occur not only by a modest process of use and disuse but by the more drastic or even violent process of mutation, not only by evolution but by revolution. It has been challenged also by our growing knowledge of the physical universe which casts doubt upon the notion that, however other things may change, "the earth abideth forever." The "everlasting hills" themselves are threatened by glacial drift, fire and flood, earthquakes and cosmic explosions. They are even threatened today by the possibility of man-made explosions which can, in their awful immensity, destroy the earth as the home of man.

It is against some such background that one must consider our changing world. First of all, we should note a radical change in the nature and rate of change itself. Among subhuman species change occurs almost entirely through "physically transmitted systems of nucleo-proteins." With man, as Julian Huxley has said, "in one out of the million or so animal species mind developed to a stage at which it gave its possessor the power for true speech and conceptual thought. . . . With this, a new method of evolutionary change was introduced—cumulative change . . . by mentally transmitted systems alone. Man thus became "the spearhead of [a new] evolutionary process on earth." *

Cultural diffusion and social change

Unique among all the myriad forms of life—man alone developed a culture and a civilization. Since, however, the geographical limits of any civilization are determined by the available means of transpor-

* See *New Bottles for New Wine*, New York: Harper, 1957, pp. 102–103.

tation and communication, the forces of change for centuries were narrowly circumscribed and moved but slowly from one community to another. Even within a single community new ideas, new inventions, new patterns of thought and behavior were confined to narrow elites and seeped downward and outward only as molasses moves through sandstone. Consider, for example, the fact that from the invention of the horse-drawn chariot around 3000 B.C. to the coming of the steam engine there was little change in the speed or comfort of land transportation. An Englishman of A.D. 1700 had few if any advantages over an Egyptian of 1700 B.C. As late as 1895, when Samuel Morse traveled from Washington, D.C., to his wife's funeral in New Haven, Connecticut, it took him seven days. No faster than Nebuchadnezzar, Caesar, Charlemagne, or Napoleon. If the available means of transportation were slow, so, too, were the channels of human communication. Smoke signals, tribal drums, the semaphore flag, were improvements on the foot messenger or the Pony Express, but today, of course, communication signals move with the speed of light.

The revolutionary changes in modes of communication and transportation that have occurred within the last century and a half have not only induced changes on their own account but have vastly increased the rate and scope of change itself.* A child born even a hundred years ago could have awakened in colonial America or, for that matter, in ancient Assyria or Babylon and recognized the essential conditions of life as not too different from his own. Not so with the child of today. No man today, according to Margaret Mead, can die in the culture to which he was born. So numerous are the changes occurring almost daily in the condition of his life and so swiftly do they pass from elites to masses, from community to community, continent to continent, that he scarcely has time to adjust to one before another is upon him. Never before has the rate of change been so great in nearly every aspect of human life. Problems of understanding and adaptation no longer are merely periodic or cyclical but continuous. "Condense, if you will," said President Kennedy, "the fifty thousand years of man's recorded

* Consider travel speeds of a century ago as compared to the supersonic flights of today, let alone the rate at which contemporary space craft encircle the globe.

Consider, also, that as late as 1899 the *Scientific American* reported an estimated 7,000 motor vehicles in Europe, of which over 5,000 were in France, 268 in Germany, 90 in Austria-Hungary, 90 in Belgium, 44 in Spain, 304 in Great Britain, 111 in Italy, 68 in Holland, and 114 in Switzerland. "It is impossible," said the editor, "to state how many automobiles are in this country; [i.e., the United States]. It is estimated the number is 500. We think that 300 or 350 would be a nearer figure."

Scientific American, September, 1899. In 1963 there were over 80 million motor vehicles registered in the United States.

history [into] . . . half a century. . . . [On such a scale] [a]bout ten years ago . . . man emerged from his cave . . . five years ago man learned to write. . . . Last month, [came] electric lights and telephones and automobiles and airplanes. Only last week . . . nuclear power. And now if America's new spacecraft succeeds in reaching Venus, we will have literally reached the stars before midnight tonight." *

The invention of invention: the knowledge explosion

Never before have organized scientific and scholarly research, formal education, and planned technological development loomed so large as basic factors in the transformation of our world. It is not only the inventions that flow in a torrential flood from fertile minds *but the invention of invention itself* that marks the revolution of modern time. In earlier days the isolation of the scientist and scholar reduced the rate at which new ideas moved from the library and laboratory to the market place. Plutarch tells an amusing but significant story about Archimedes that illustrates this isola-

* From Mortimer Adler and Robert M. Hutchins (eds.), *Great Ideas Today,* 1963 (Chicago: Encyclopaedia Britannica, 1964), p. 84.

tion of pure from applied science. Through many ingenious inventions, Archimedes had obtained "the renown of more than human sagacity. [Yet] he would not deign to leave behind any commentary or writing on such subjects, but repudiating as sordid and ignoble the whole trade of engineering and every sort of art that lends itself to mere use . . . he placed his whole affection and ambition in those purer speculations where there can be no reference to the vulgar needs of life." This has now profoundly changed. The marriage of pure Science and Scholarship with Engineering and Statesmanship has wrought what we now call the Knowledge Explosion.

Some idea of the dimensions of this so-called Knowledge Explosion may be gathered from a few figures. In 1965 it is estimated that over 30,000 journals are being published in technical and scientific fields alone, and the number is said to be increasing at the rate of 1,000 a year. Upwards of 2 million scientific and technical articles are being published each year, plus 100,000 or more technical reports of one kind or another. Equally significant is the report of Dr. Wesley Simonton of the University of Minnesota that about 50 per cent of the scientific material now available has been published since 1950 and that 80 per cent of all the scientists the world has known are alive today.*

Optimists see on the moving frontiers of human knowledge a world purged of all the evils of tyranny and human exploitation, of poverty and social injustice, of war and famine, of disease and even death. Others see no such vision but, rather, the aggravation of current sources of discontent compounded by the possibility of self-destruction on a global scale. With Ecclesiastes, they say, "in much wisdom is much grief: and he that increaseth knowledge increaseth sorrow."

At the very least the Knowledge Explosion poses new problems as difficult as those it solves. As automation frees mankind from the ancient burdens of human toil, it generates mass unemployment at an estimated net job displacement rate as high as 40,000 a week. As medicine and the healing arts extend the span of life, they generate a Population Explosion that threatens to engulf humanity in a Malthusian tragedy of unexampled scope and severity. Rapid transportation and instantaneous communication banish time and distance and make the human race, if not a single family, at least a community of neighbors in a shrinking world. But the automobile has just about destroyed our great central cities through a new and malignant form

* See *New York Times,* Jan. 24, 1965.

of traffic sclerosis. And its exhaust fumes have polluted the urban atmosphere often beyond the limits of toleration or even survival. Industrial expansion has inundated us with an avalanche of goods but has polluted our waterways and defiled our landscapes. Radio and television, of which Telstar is but a recent development, have made it possible for the best in literature, science, and art to be accessible to tens of millions hitherto living in isolation from the main stream of contemporary culture. But what do they do to our canons of public taste? And what do they do to those precious cultural differences which have made our pluralistic world so rich and intriguing in its all but infinite variety? Are we now to become a world standardized and homogenized by mass media controlled by an oligarchy of bureaucrats, public or private?

One could go on, but these examples will do to illustrate the paradoxical nature of World Change. Even the paradox of Progress and Poverty remains, aggravated by the very forces that now make its abolition possible. For thousands of years, in one form or another, poverty has been a central feature of human life on this planet. Today, however, it has a new and greater significance in the context of our rapidly changing world.

The population explosion

For one striking consequence of the so-called Knowledge Explosion has been a Population Explosion—from which, as from Pandora's box, countless other problems rise.

At the turn of this century there were an estimated one and a half billion people in the world. Today world population is estimated at more than three billions, and the rate of increase is going up, not down. According to Kingsley Davis, world population grew by 6 per cent in each 10-year period between 1850 and 1900; by 7 per cent between 1900 and 1930; by 10 per cent between 1930 and 1950; and by an estimated 17 per cent in the decade 1950–1960. In 1965 population growth is approaching a rate of 2 per cent a year. Dr. Alvin Weinberg of the Oak Ridge National Laboratory estimates that in another millennium (i.e., by the year 3000) world population may reach one trillion. At present rates of growth, in the year 6500 population will equal the total mass of the earth itself.* To compound the problem, the explosion has been most pronounced in the so-called underdeveloped areas of the world, in Latin America, Oceania, the Middle East, Africa, and Asia.

* *Science Digest,* February, 1963.

In 1954 mainland China reported a population of 583 million. Today there are close to 700 million people in Communist China and another 450 million in India. Of the 50 million or more people added to the world's population each year, one half are in Asia. In 1900 there were only two Asians for each European; by the year 2000 (i.e., 35 years from now) this ratio will be four Asians to one European.

This Population Explosion, viewed against the so-called *revolution of rising expectations* in the underdeveloped areas of the world, offers one key to world politics in 1965 and the years ahead. At the very time when the burgeoning populations of Latin America, Asia, Africa, and the Middle East are upsetting the population balance of the world, the peoples of these areas are demanding better standards of living, more education, more of all the good things of life, and above all they are demanding equality as human beings, to be treated not merely with kindness and toleration but with dignity and respect.* And these demands are not un-

* A recent study by Professor Hadley Cantril of the Institute for International Social Research—has attempted to identify and measure the aspirations of people in a number of countries, including the United States, Cuba, Brazil, the Philippines, Israel, West Germany, Panama, the Dominican Republic, Poland, Yugoslavia, Nigeria, and India. Almost everywhere they include hope for a better standard of living, access to health and medical care for themselves and their families, better opportunities

related to changes in patterns of transportation and communication which have brought to otherwise remote regions of the world the ideas of the American Declaration of Independence, the French and English Bills of Rights, and knowledge of the unbelievable affluence of the peoples of Europe and America.*

Unfortunately the scientific and technological revolution which has produced this Population Explosion has so far failed to meet the insistent demand of people in these areas for a better life. As Eugene Staley of the Stanford Research Institute has said, "Despite all the vaunted technological

---

for education and development for their children, mutual respect, and a sense of personal worth.

See *Scientific American,* February, 1963, for a summary of the methods used in this study. The complete study was being published by Rutgers University Press at the time this essay was being written.

* Even the affluent United States shows pockets or levels of poverty hard to reconcile with the economic and technological possibilities present in American society although the extent of such poverty depends a great deal on how the term is defined. In comparison with the poor in underdeveloped countries, the number so described in this country would be small. But if we include those with incomes less than enough to support a reasonable standard of health and decency in the United States, the estimated number of poor people varies from as high as 90 million to a low of 20 million, in either case a sufficiently large proportion of our total population to give more than academic interest to President Johnson's "War on Poverty." See Michael Harrington, *The Other America* (New York: Macmillan, 1962). Also *United States News and World Report,* "Poverty—U.S.A.," Feb. 17, 1964.

and economic progress of modern times, there are probably more poverty-stricken people in the world today than there were fifty years ago." We ought not, therefore, to be surprised if Asian, African, and Middle Eastern opinion moves toward radical remedies to relieve their distress. In the world-wide contest for the allegiance of these areas, political ideologies will play an important role; but, barring catastrophic wars and revolutions, propaganda of the deed will be more effective than propaganda of the word alone.

The new nationalism—
A twentieth-century anachronism

Translating the demands of these underdeveloped areas into political terms, their leaders have set a high priority on political independence. One by one, the great colonial empires have been undermined or overthrown.* The result has been a multiplication of nation-states unlike anything in previous history. The United Nations began its career with 51 members. In planning its headquarters

* In the Cantril study of aspiration levels, it is significant to note that "when people have a sense that they are successful participants in a national political movement, there is an appreciable relation between the ratings they assign to their personal situation and to that of their country." *Scientific American,* February, 1963.

building in New York it made provision for an eventual 75. In 1965 facilities had to be expanded to accommodate 113 members (a number temporarily reduced to 112 when Zanzibar and Tanganyika merged under a single flag), a 100 per cent increase since 1945.

In the old League of Nations only 6 out of 54 member states were from Asia and Africa—about 10 per cent. Today Asia and Africa claim 56 members—50 per cent of the total. When one reflects that in the UN Assembly each member state—regardless of its size—has one vote, one can discern in the changing composition a significant shift in the balance of power, a shift that would be more dramatic and significant if the new nations were, in fact, true nation-states and if formal political independence were more closely related to real political power. The fact is, of course, that many of the new states lack the resources, both natural and human, that have come to be regarded as essential to any viable political community. The result is that many of them are nations in name only, destined for many years to come to be junior partners or satellites of more powerful neighbors or allies.

In all this we confront another paradox of our changing world. Political independence and self-determination of nations have been cardinal principles of modern democratic theory. In the American system of values they have had high priority. It was the American Revolution that set in motion the world-wide revolt against colonialism —and sent the slogans of self-government, freedom, and equality ringing around the world. The full harvest of these ideas has now come. Unhappily, as the tide of nationalism rises to its flood, its demographic, economic, scientific, and technological foundations have begun to crumble.

In an agrarian society it was possible to encompass within the jurisdiction of a single nation the land area, population, and natural resources necessary to maintain national independence and a viable political economy. The system was never ideal, and resources rarely corresponded to national needs or aspirations. But for 150 years or more the system worked fairly well until two world wars, not to mention half a dozen minor ones, within a single generation emphasized how fragile and unstable the structure was.

As we look out upon the world of 1965, it would seem self-evident that the Knowledge Explosion with its quasi-logarithmic rate of change has made the current nationalistic explosion a political anachronism. Does this mean that the nation-state is obsolete? I think not necessarily. The nation-state, when thought of in terms of cultural and, even within limits, political and economic autonomy, can, it seems to me, continue to contribute significantly to human freedom and welfare. Nevertheless, as science and technology devour both space and time, rich and affluent nations, like rich and affluent people within nations, will find it more and more difficult to live in splendid isolation from the poor and the neglected. The United Nations with all its weaknesses has offered a forum in which so-called underdeveloped nations and peoples can be heard through representatives of their own choosing. Their attempts to translate aspirations into reality are reflected in the work of some fourteen specialized agencies from UNESCO to the World Bank, and in their covenants against genocide and for an International Charter of Human Rights.

What is obvious is that if we are to maintain peace and promote the freedom and welfare of the human race we must look to new forms of political organization. We must, in short, create a world community or a world civilization if we are to save our own nation and our own civilization from the decline and fall that have characterized other nations and other civilizations in the past. The scientific and technological instruments for such a world community are at hand. Even the political instruments are beginning to emerge although we continue to see them only as through a glass darkly.

The solution obviously is not to be found in offensive and defensive alliances among 112 sovereign states. Nor is it to be found in the Bipolarization of political power, with peace dependent on a balance of nuclear terror. The first has been tried and found wanting—and the second is even now falling apart. Enormous cracks have appeared in the erstwhile monolithic power structure of the communist world. And on the other side—where a monolithic power structure and ideology were never very clear—there are signs of dissent if not dissension, of which de Gaulle is but a symbol.

The end of Bipolarism

The fact seems to be that Bipolarism is being succeeded by what is called Polycentrism—a world composed of not one or two but many power systems able to speak and, within limits, to act independently of what Moscow, Washington, or Peiping may wish.

However much the ideologues on both sides may deplore all this, the gradual erosion of the bipolar power structure can be a step forward in our search for a world political community. In the first place, it has helped to mitigate the tensions arising from the Cold War. It has already demonstrated that legitimate national aspirations based on different cultural and political interests cannot permanently be subordinated to the national or ideological interests of one or another superpower. But it has also demonstrated that eighteenth- and nineteenth-century nationalism is an anachronism, incompatible with the kind of world political community in which not only legitimate national interest but individual freedom and welfare can be secure.

For many years to come, no doubt, the national state will continue to be the only power structure vested with legitimate authority to employ physical coercion to protect and advance its interests. We are a long way from the day when this authority will be transferred to a world government. The so-called Community of Nations is still pretty much in that "state of nature" which Thomas Hobbes described three hundred years ago. "Hereby it is manifest," he wrote, "that during the time men live without a common power to keep them all in awe, they are in that condition which is called War, and such a War is of every man against every man. [And in such a state of nature, he continued] Men live in continual fear and danger of violent death, and the life of man is solitary, poor, nasty, brutish and short." Yet there are steps already taken which point in a direction which may make escape from this state of nature possible. Although the United Nations is a long way from becoming a world government, it has nevertheless been vested with a limited authority to use coercion in situations threatening the peace of the world. The limited United Nations police actions in Korea, in the Middle East, in the Congo, and more recently in Cyprus are less significant in themselves than as symbols of the shape of things to come.

Toward a world society

These peacemaking actions were made possible after 1950 by the adoption of what has been called the Uniting for Peace Resolution by the United Nations Assembly. By this resolution important decision-making powers were assumed by the Assembly. Unlike the Security Council, where the single vote of one of the five permanent members can defeat a proposal, the Assembly acts by majority vote, each member, regardless of size, having a single vote.

It has been this transfer of decision-making power to the Assembly and the ensuing peacekeeping activities in various parts of the world that brought on the financial crisis of the United Nations in 1965. France and the U.S.S.R., among the great powers, refused to pay their share of the cost of these operations—because they had not been authorized by the Security Council, where, as I have said, they would be subject to veto by the single vote of any one of the five permanent members—France, United States of America, U.S.S.R., United Kingdom, and China.

Under Article 19 a member failing to pay its share of the costs of United Nations operations may be denied its vote. Faced with the refusal of the U.S.S.R., France, and some nine other members to pay their assessments for these peacekeeping operations and the reluctance of other members to enforce Article 19, the United Nations was virtually brought to a standstill in the 1965 sessions. Unless this conflict over the authority of the Assembly to authorize such peacekeeping operations is resolved, the United Nations may be seriously crippled. It cannot, I believe, be destroyed.

The United Nations is not the only sign of a new world struggling to be born. The outlawing of war as an instrument of national policy and the move toward some form of international control of nuclear weapons are others. Ultimately some form of world government endowed with authority to use force to maintain peace among nations, as the legitimate governments of the world now employ force to maintain peace within those borders, is essential.

In the meantime new forms of political organization and behavior are already beginning to emerge. One need only contrast the position of the United States following World War I with that following World War II. From a professed policy of isolation and no permanent entangling alliances, we find ourselves bound by treaty arrangements that have drawn us not only into the United Nations but into nearly every region on the globe. Our policy of foreign aid has made us a partner in the economic development and military defense of half the nations of the world. Between 1948 and 1964 upward of $100 billion had been made available for assistance in Europe, the Far East, the Middle East and South Asia, Africa and Latin America. "One of the brightest pages of the world's history," said President Kennedy, "has been the . . . programs this country has devised . . . to help free people achieve economic development and the control of their own destinies."

Equally important has been the application of the American principle of federal government to the development of supranational regional authorities in Africa, the West Indies, South East Asia, and, most dramatically, in Europe, where a

Common Market, a Common Defense Community, and a Council of Europe have developed.

It may well be that the European example illustrates an inevitable trend toward other regional arrangements in other areas of the world looking toward a number of federal unions—as intermediate way stations on the road to a world community with a world government of its own.

Politics and social change in the United States

Time forbids even random comment on the impact of world change on the internal affairs of the United States. We, too, have felt the effects of the Knowledge Explosion and a spectacular increase in population.* As the world shrinks under the impact of science and technology, foreign policy moves to the center of the stage. Indeed the line between foreign and domestic policy all but disappears. Some three fourths of our national budget in one way or another goes for international affairs and now constitutes a critically important factor in our gross national product. Whatever we do in education, scientific research, social welfare,

* The Census Bureau has recently estimated a population of nearly 270 million for the United States by 1985—just twenty years from now. This estimate, the Bureau observes, is "based on a slightly declining birth rate in line with the trend of recent years." *New York Times*, Feb. 27, 1965.

race relations, has its effect upon our world image as that image is in turn affected by events in distant lands. Moreover, population trends visible elsewhere are also visible here with similar consequences. A rapidly expanding population with increasing proportions both under fifteen and over sixty-five, with increasingly specialized skills, and increasing in density and mobility, is everywhere accompanied by a disproportionate increase in the role of government in human affairs. So long as these trends continue, those who long for less government and lower taxes are likely to be disappointed. Moreover, the increasing centralization of our economy and the continued acceleration of transportation and communications will inevitably result in increasing centralization of government with an expanding executive establishment. Not the least of these effects will be a meteoric increase in the role of education with consequences for us that I cannot even begin to explore.

These are but a few items of commentary on our changing world as it looks to me in April, 1965. You will note that I have made no mention of the Negro revolt in this country and its implications for both domestic and foreign policy. But what is one to say? The deep South, since the Civil War, has suffered from arrested development, and the Negro's struggle for civil rights is part of the

South's struggle for economic development and political integration with the rest of the nation. The spectacular growth of the rest of the nation has, until very recently, bypassed the states of the Confederacy, which for all practical purposes have comprised our major underdeveloped area. Not the least of the factors which go to explain this is the racial problem. The availability of an abundant, illiterate, servile, but inefficient labor force—complicated by racial segregation in nearly every aspect of economic and racial life—has deprived the Southern states of the initiative, energy, and drive that have characterized their Northern and Western neighbors. And this has been true at the very time when throughout the world economic and social progress has come increasingly to depend on literacy, technical training, and intellectual development. Recently enacted Civil Rights legislation may be a bitter pill for many Southern leaders to swallow. But in the end they, too, will see it as a major step in the moral as well as the economic and political regeneration of their section. And I hope it is unnecessary to point up the significance of the nationwide Negro demand for the freedom and equality of opportunity long enjoyed by their white neighbors. A large majority of the world's population is colored—and what happens here to our own large colored minority will speak much more loudly to the people of Africa and Asia than almost anything we can say. The Civil Rights Act is thus a major step in persuading the rest of the world that we do in fact believe that all men are created equal and that we will treat them as equals, with mutual forbearance, understanding, and respect.

New Canons for old

How can I at this point summarize what I have been trying to say? Perhaps the best summary is one provided for me by my friend Lynn White—formerly President of Mills College and now Professor of History at U.C.L.A. The old world, he points out, i.e., the world of fifty or a hundred years ago, was governed by certain cultural canons which in our day and age have radically changed. First was the *Canon of the Occident,* which confined our view of the world largely to the West and to Western Civilization. Second was the *Canon of logic and language,* which limited our training in analysis and communication largely to the logical principles of Aristotle and the languages of Latin, Greek, and Western Europe. Third was the *Canon of rationality,* that "reason is the supreme human attribute" and that anything nonrational or nonlogical was somehow not worthy of man and his heritage. Fourth was the *Canon of the hierarchy of values,* which assumed not only that our values were good and others' therefore bad—but that within our system of values some types of human activity were more worthy of reverence than others. A life of contemplation and prayer was conceived to be superior to one of labor and love.

In place of these Canons we have (1) The *Canon of the globe,* which has displaced the *Canon of the Occident.* We no longer talk about East is East and West is West and never the twain shall meet. They have met and are now in process of merging. And we now are reaching for the Moon. (2) The *Canon of symbols* has replaced the *Canon of logic and language.* "We are," says Professor White, "beginning to see that the distinctive thing about the human species is that we are a symbol making animal." Emancipated from Aristotelian logic and Western European languages, we have created new and exciting symbols to name and describe a hundred new ideas and concepts, and we have learned that languages other than those of the West are not only worthy of our study but can be vehicles of communication to hundreds of millions formerly beyond our reach. (3) The *Canon of rationality* has been profoundly modified by the *Canon of the unconscious.* No small part of human behavior we now realize is rooted in unconscious motives and unconscious drives—and that nonrational conduct may be an essential component of any stable civilization. I am reminded in this connection of a poem by Ogden Nash that goes as follows:

When geniuses all in every nation
Hasten us toward obliteration,
Perhaps it will take the dolts and geese
*To drag us backward into peace.**

(4) Finally the *Canon of the hierarchy of values* has been amended by the *Canon of a spectrum of values,* which recognizes that in a pluralistic world men may have different value systems which are not either right or wrong but merely different.

The old order changeth

In this new world, we in America stand not so much on the threshold of great changes as in a moving stream of continuous change whose rate of flow increases every day. "Our life has broken away from the past," said Woodrow Wilson. "The life of America is not the life that it was twenty years ago; it is not the life that it was ten years ago.

* From "The Miraculous Countdown" in *Everyone But Thee and Me* (Boston: Little, Brown & Co., 1962, 3d printing), p. 86.

We have changed our economic conditions . . . from top to bottom. . . . The old political formulas do not fit the present problems; they read now like documents taken out of a forgotten age. . . . The old order changeth—changeth under our very eyes, not quietly and equitably, but swiftly and with the noise and heat and tumult of reconstruction." *

If this was true in 1912, how much more true it is in 1965. Nations and civilizations, like individual organisms, must somehow adapt to change or die, and we are no exception. Perhaps in the process we shall find, with T. S. Eliot, that

> *We shall not cease from explorations*
> *And the end of all our exploring*
> *Will be to arrive where we started*
> *And know the place for the first time.*†

In any case, it is well to be reminded again and again that

> No man is an Iland, intire of itselfe: every man is a peece of the Continent, a part of the maine; if a Clod bee washed away by the Sea, Europe is the

* From *The New Freedom* (New York: Doubleday, Page & Co., 1914), pp. 3–5, 29.

† From "Little Gidding" in "The Four Quartets," *Complete Poems and Plays* (New York: Harcourt, Brace, 1952), p. 145.

lesse . . . any man's death diminishes me, because I am involved in Mankinde; And therefore never send to know for whom the bell tolls; it tolls for thee.*

* From John Donne, *Devotions,* XVII.

II

Political science: knowledge for what?

"The greatest and fairest sort of wisdom by far," said Plato, "is that which is concerned with the ordering of states." Like other branches of human knowledge, the study of politics has passed through various stages from magic and superstition to something approaching a positive science; and its achievements both of theory and of practice have been considerable.

The late Nicholas Murray Butler of Columbia once said that nothing had been added to our knowledge of politics not to be found in the writings of Aristotle and Plato. This is manifestly untrue although the statement poses a problem to which I shall want to return later in this discourse. For the present, it is enough to point to the theory and practice of representative government, the federal system, the doctrine of equity in the administration of justice—not to mention parliamentary government, judicial review, and the American presidency—to indicate that President Butler was more modest on our behalf than he need have been. Moreover, with all due respect to the ancients, I think we know more today about the nature, basis, and structure of political power than they did and a great deal more about human nature and politics, administrative organization and management, crime and punishment, international relations, and comparative government. And what is even more important, I think, we know more about the application of scientific method to the problems of government and politics than did our honored forebears of ancient times.

Emergence of political science

But before offering a bill of particulars on these matters we might look briefly at the evolution of political science as a major branch of human knowledge. The systematic study of politics has its roots in primitive recognition of the importance of political power in every organized human society. Recognition led to speculation concerning the nature, structure, and scope of power and the search for some principle of nature, religion, or ethics to make it legitimate. It was Aristotle who noted that man is by nature a political animal, that only a beast or a god can survive outside of political society, and that somewhere in that society there must be lodged the right, within the bounds of legitimacy, to use force to maintain order. But long before Aristotle, men in the most primitive societies were conscious of political power as a fact of life, for, in the words of John Austin, they were accustomed to giving habitual obedience to a government of some kind. Recognition of this fact led to efforts to legitimatize and rationalize the prevailing power structure. These efforts produced ideas as primitive as the notion of Thrasymachus that "Might is Right," that Power is its own excuse, and other explanations redolent of magic and superstition. The literature of anthropology is full of examples of primitive power structures rationalized by elaborate myths attributing magical origin and supernatural powers to tribal chiefs.*

* In his novel *Hawaii,* James Michener describes how the sacred *Mana* (a kind of divine grace and power) flowed from the

From such beginnings it was only a step to more elaborate notions of divine right in those who rule, a type of doctrine that has not yet run its course even in many advanced cultures. Obviously when God's will and the will of those who govern are identified as one and the same, disobedience or resistance to established authority becomes not merely subversive but sacrilegious. "Submit yourselves to the higher powers," said St. Paul, "for the powers that be are ordained of God."

But divine right as a rationalization for political power was challenged by religion itself when the church or the true believer, as a person, appealed to a divine law to which even kings and potentates must bow. It was indeed the resistance of the church and the true believer to the godlike claims of kings and tyrants that paved the way for the most common contemporary rationalization of political power as finding its only legitimate source in the consent of the governed. The rituals of political power may still reflect the notion that all legitimate authority derives from God's will—but the discovery of God's will has moved from the mind of a hereditary monarch or aristocracy to

---

gods to the kings of Hawaii and from the kings to their people. Hence to touch the person of the king or even to step on his shadow was tabu lest the king lose *Mana* to those not worthy to receive it.

that of an elected representative body, or the will of the people as expressed directly at the polls. The basis of political power has thus returned to what no doubt has always been its actual source, the consent of the governed.

The structure of power

As men have reflected on the *nature* of political power and have sought some acceptable principle for ensuring its legitimacy, so, too, have they reflected on the proper *structure* of power and the limits within which and the purposes for which it may legitimately be used. The rule of the one, the few, and the many as describing the various ways in which power may be structured has been recogized at least since Herodotus. It has been the theme of political speculation from Aristotle and Plato to Machiavelli and Montesquieu, and from Thomas Hobbes and John Locke to Alexander Hamilton and James Madison. It remains a basic problem today in discussions of governmental forms not only in the new states of Africa and Asia but in the U.S.S.R., Western Europe, the United States of America, and the United Nations.

Similarly, problems of structure and form, as well as of the scope and process of power, are at the heart of discussions concerning both intra- and intergovernmental relations—discussions that have a continuous history reaching from Thucydides and Polybius, John Locke and the Founding Fathers of the American Constitution, to the Kestnbaum Report of 1955. For discussions of structure and form reflect basic theories concerning the proper role not only of executive, legislative, and judicial powers but also of central and local authorities in the total process of government. No one can realistically look at the process of government and remain indifferent to its form and structure.

Structure and process

In the evolution of political science men have alternated in their emphasis on form and structure, on one hand, and process, on the other, forgetting that there is an integral relation between them. One cannot talk meaningfully of "due process of law," "due notice and a fair hearing," "trial by jury," without reference to the legal or administrative structures through which these procedures are applied in particular cases. Nor can one understand the legislative, administrative, or judicial process apart from the institutions to which these processes relate. The decision-making process upon which so much contemporary research is focused does not occur in a vacuum or in outer space but within the context of an institutional structure that affects it just as that structure is in turn affected by the process which it seeks to contain. One may note also that the complex procedures by which the consent of the governed is given to public authority require the organization and management of reasonably stable institutions, including organized factions, pressure groups, political parties, ballots, polling booths, electoral colleges, and so forth. And it is obvious that the form and structure of these institutions has an important and often decisive effect upon the process of government.

The scope of power

Another among the persistent problems of political science is the proper *scope* of political power. What is the proper relation between the state and society, between political authority and the individual, as well as those innumerable voluntary or private associations through which individuals enter social relations? In primitive societies, as indeed in the ancient Greek city-state, political power reached to the outermost limits and most intimate aspects of the human condition.* Distinc-

* "What distinguished the Greek polis [city-state]," says Lewis Mumford, ". . . was the fact that no part of its life was

tions between the proper sphere of state and society were obscure when they were made at all, and political authority was essentially totalitarian in theory if not in practice. Individuals as such, as beings apart from and independent of the political community, were unknown. The organized community, and the individual only as the micro-image of that community, was the bearer of values. The individual as an entity, as a creature having thoughts and feelings, and even rights, apart and even different from those of the community, was a revolutionary idea. The emergence of the idea that the individual could be a bearer of values —an end in itself and not merely a means to an end—posed a political problem of such magnitude that it threatened to destroy—and in the end did destroy—primitive society and the ancient political community.

Political pluralism

But before this could occur it was necessary to establish the integrity of the individual and the rights and privileges of social groups as intermediary between the political community and the

---

out of sight or out of mind. . . . All that men did was open to inspection. . . ." From *The City in History* (New York: Harcourt, Brace, 1961), p. 165.

individual. In the process there emerged a pluralistic society, with a private power structure of groups and associations serving individual citizens and competing with the political or public power structure for their allegiance. In time they came to rival and almost to displace the political state itself. In due course, however, the supremacy of the political state was established, although not with the amplitude of power which had characterized many primitive societies or the ancient political community. Although Thomas Hobbes, the philosopher of absolutism, compared such voluntary groups to "worms in the entrails of man," absolute monarchs were compelled to recognize their existence and to accord them a certain degree of autonomy in the political community. But in the process many ancient and traditional ties were dissolved, and from the autonomous group the autonomous individual appeared as the forerunner of what Emil Lederer has called "the State of the Masses." In this state the restraints imposed by semiautonomous associations decline and both voluntary groups and the emergent individuals are again absorbed into a totalitarian political community.

During the whole of this long and often painful process political scientists have sought to understand, describe, rationalize, accelerate, or resist events as they transpired. Indeed, it is in the research and reflections of men like Plato and Aristotle, Cicero and Polybius, Marsiglio of Padua, and John of Salisbury, Machiavelli, Hobbes, Locke, and Rousseau, that the shifting patterns of political power find their best expression and rationalization.

Means and ends

But these great architects of political science were more than political taxonomists concerned only with the structure and process of government and the limits or scope of political power. They were also concerned with the uses to which political power is put—not alone with the ways and means of an ordered society but with its ends as well. Indeed, to Aristotle the acid test of a well-ordered state was the degree to which it served the common good. The form and structure of power were less important than the ends it was contrived to serve. It was not the rule of one man, or of a few, that made tyranny and oligarchy evil but their use of power for selfish or private rather than social or public ends—for the special interest of a family or a faction rather than for the common good of all. Various patterns of power structure and process were recognized as legitimate means for the discovery of measures best calculated to promote the common good.

Conceptions of the common good, however, and of the most appropriate ways to discover and to serve it varied considerably. Plato thought of it as best secured in a stratified society with each man, in F. H. Bradley's phrase, finding, or being assigned to, his proper station and its duties. Hobbes thought of it as *Peace,* secured by a monopoly of violence in an Absolute Monarch, the sign and symbol of the great Leviathan. Locke defined it as the protection of property and persons from arbitrary rule. John S. Mill, Jeremy Bentham, and the Utilitarians said the common good was the greatest good to the greatest number—as measured by a calculus of pleasure and pain. And the Founding Fathers of the American Constitution, among the most astute of political theorists and practitioners, sought to make the concept of the common good and the means for its discovery and fulfillment reasonably explicit in the Constitution. To promote a more perfect union, establish justice, insure domestic tranquillity, provide for the common defense, promote the general welfare, and insure the blessings of liberty—were, as they thought, the major components of the common good. To discover and secure these ends they established a government armed with great power yet limited to certain ways and means, and controlled by well-defined procedures, to prevent its arbitrary use.

The point I wish to make is that from the beginning of any systematic study of political science men have been concerned with ends as well as means, with policy as well as structure and process. To nearly all of the great political philosophers who have contributed most to its development, a "value free" political science would have seemed absurd—a contradiction in terms. If, as David Easton has said, politics is a process for the authoritative allocation of values in society, a political scientist indifferent to the value problems of his own time is blind to the only materials that give any meaning or significance to his discipline. But more on this hereafter.

The political philosophers

In the evolution of political science one can discover a number of frames of reference from which these problems have been viewed, each with its own techniques or methods of study. Among these one can distinguish philosophical, historical, legal or jurisprudential, administrative, and behavioral frames of reference. The contributions of philosophers to our knowledge of political science are immeasurable. Their names constitute a roster of what can only be called Political Science's Hall of Fame. Aristotle and Plato, St. Thomas and Spinoza, Machiavelli and Melanchthon, Marsiglio and John of Salisbury, Hobbes and Locke, Hume and Kant, Hegel, Descartes and Comte, Mill, Bentham, and John Dewey are but a partial list. As philosophers their methods of study have been reflection and introspection, inductive and deductive logic, tested by a crude empiricism. The Cartesian revolution had its effect on political science as on mathematics and natural science.* And who can measure our debt to Hobbes and Locke and Hume for laying the foundations of modern political psychology, or to the pragmatists and the legal positivists for exploding many a time-honored political myth?

The political historians

Second to the philosophers have been those who study politics from a historical frame of reference:

* The novelty of Descartes's method, according to A. D. Lindsay, "consisted in the rejection of the syllogism and the affirmation of the truth that the discoveries of reason are not made by deducing the particular from the universal, but from perceiving the universal in the individual instance." (From Descartes, *Discourse on Method* [New York: E. P. Dutton, Everyman's ed., 1912] p. xv.)

Descartes's method, as he himself described it, was to "reduce involved and obscure propositions step by step to those that are simpler and then . . . attempt to ascend to the knowledge of all others by precisely similar steps." (*Ibid.*, p. xvi.)

Herodotus and Thucydides, Tacitus, Plutarch, and Polybius, Buckle, Hume, Grote, and Gibbon, not to mention Fortescue, Bishop Stubbs, Pollock and Maitland, von Gierke, de Tocqueville, Trevelyan, and dozens more among Europeans. In the United States a good many of our leading political scientists were historians, or perhaps one should say a good many historians were political scientists. One thinks at once of men like Bradford and Winthrop, Hutchinson and Fiske, Bancroft, Turner, Beard, Osgood, Parrington, Rhodes, McIlwain, Dunning, and others. Hutchinson's *History of Massachusetts,* Fiske's *American Revolution,* Bancroft's *History of the United States,* were mainly concerned with politics. Turner's essay on the *Frontier* was, in fact, a treatise in political theory, as de Tocqueville's *Ancient Regime* and *Democracy in America* were studies in political sociology. Hannis Taylor's *Origin and Growth of the American Constitution,* McMaster's essay, *With the Fathers,* Learned's history of *The President's Cabinet,* Farrand's *Records of the Federal Constitution,* Elliot's *Debates on the . . . Constitution,* not to mention the work of J. Allen Smith, Charles Beard, and Forrest MacDonald, are as much political science as history. An early study of pressure politics in a revolutionary context was Arthur Schlesinger, Sr.'s *Colonial Merchants in the American Revolution;* and Mc-

Ilwain's books on *Constitutionalism*, the *American Revolution*, and the *High Court of Parliament* were as much studies in constitutional law as in history. Others like Woodrow Wilson, Dunning, Merriam, and Allan Nevins were essentially political scientists using history as a vehicle for discussing political ideas and institutions. There are many others writing from a historical frame of reference both in this country and abroad who have enriched our knowledge of political science. Indeed, for a long time—and in many places even today—political science has been, as it were, in bondage to history and historians.

Public law

Supplementing the work of political philosophers and historians have been students of public law. Charles Beard used to complain about our servitude to the lawyers—to Montesquieu, Coke, Bracton, Blackstone, Vinogradoff, Dicey, Duguit, Esmein, Verdross, and Kelsen among Europeans, and in the United States to Chancellor Kent, Brinton Coxe, Charles Haines, T. R. Powell, E. S. Corwin, and John Dickinson, not to mention Marshall, Taney, Holmes, and Brandeis. Our debt to the lawyers is a great one, for it was they who not only developed the principle of constitutional government but through courts and administrative tribunals made them something more than a "brooding omnipresence in the sky." Indeed, public law as a discipline became the bridle by which the great Leviathan was to be guided and controlled. For many years public law and jurisprudence were virtually synonymous with political science.

Administration as political science

But constitutions and laws, it was recognized, are not self-enforcing. To speak of a government of laws and not of men—as constitutional lawyers loved to do—was to imply that it was the harness and not the horse that drew the cart. Hence political scientists turned their attention increasingly to the study of administration as the dynamic force in the process of government. They took to quoting Alexander Pope's couplet:

> *For forms of government let fools contest;*
> *Whate'er is best administer'd is best.*

They attacked the ancient tripartite division of government into legislative, executive, and judicial functions as unrealistic, cumbersome, and lacking in empirical validity. The whole process of government, it was said, had but two faces—Policy and

Administration—which stood toward each other in the relation of Ends and Means. Moreover, it was argued, that whatever the ends for which governments were instituted, Constitutions framed or laws enacted, nothing in fact was accomplished except through administration. In the lexicon of this administrative state, political science became synonymous with the study of administration. Principles of public administration, comparative administration, organization and management, personnel administration, budgeting and fiscal administration, state and municipal administration, international administration, judicial administration—these and other similar courses of study began to appear and to proliferate in college and university bulletins. As a bridge between the lawyers and the administrators, administrative law became a required course, at least for graduate majors in political science. So popular did the new creed become and so numerous were its disciples that a new association and a new journal, the American Society for Public Administration and the *Public Administration Review*, were established—which it was believed would rival, if not replace, the American Political Science Association and the *American Political Science Review*. Thus the child threatened to swallow up its parent or, to change the metaphor, the tail to wag the dog.

Strongly influenced by logical positivism, however, the new science of administration threatened to develop a scholasticism of its own. But a closer look at the process as well as the structure of public power saved the discipline from this fate.

The responsibilities of administration compelled political scientists to take account of a wide variety of skills and scientific disciplines employed in the public service. The "black-coated proletariat" of clerks and scribes that in the eighteenth century made up the civil service was gradually replaced by an army of highly skilled specialists representing virtually every scientific discipline from astronomy to zoology. The expansion and specialization of the public service soon made the science of administration of central importance in the process of government. The so-called Managerial Revolution of modern times is essentially a by-product of specialized skills plus large-scale organization. It is upon management's skill in mobilizing thousands of specialized civil servants toward common objectives that all Big Government depends. The administrator, in a word, became a specialist in the recruitment and management of other specialists. In doing so he was compelled to search for some frame of reference that could apply to large numbers of people having different interests, skills, and responsibilities but intent upon a common goal.

The Behavioralists

The political philosopher, historian, or constitutional lawyer could look at government as from a lofty eminence. The administrator had to see it in operation, to look at the horse as well as the harness, at political dynamics as well as political statics. He had, in a word, to focus on political behavior in all of its infinite variety. In the process he learned that political behavior, like other forms of behavior, is profoundly affected by the individual's role and status in society or what he conceives that role and status to be. A policeman in uniform on his beat, a soldier in uniform on duty, a judge on the bench, a worker in the shop or on an assembly line, a union shop steward on the job, a corporation executive—all of these and countless others display patterns of behavior and of thought associated with the specialized roles they play in the culture or subculture, system or subsystem to which they belong. The process of government is thus seen as a complex of interpersonal, intergroup, intersystem relations characterized by tension, conflict, and/or accommodation. The result is seen as a more or less stable equilibrium among all those individuals, groups, and systems that make up the public and private power structures, respectively—an equilibrium identified as Public Order if not tranquillity. To discover structures and procedures that will afford maximum opportunity for change within any established order without destroying this existing equilibrium became a major problem of government and political science.

This behavioral approach to the study of political science has not been confined to public administration. Indeed, it has its deepest roots and greatest vogue among those whose special interests lie in the study of political parties, pressure groups, voting behavior, and public opinion—i.e., with consent or consensus and with policy as well as administration. The expression of preferences among alternatives (i.e., voting), whether in the market place, at the polls, in legislative assemblies, administrative boards, and even courts of law, is now seen as the heart of the decision-making process and, hence, virtually synonymous with the political process in democratic societies. To understand voting behavior, therefore, is to come close to understanding politics in the modern world. Moreover, since the expression of preferences in a competitive market is simply another form of voting, studies of behavior in the market place, it was assumed, could throw light on many of the most important problems of government. It is not surprising, therefore, that the behavioral frame of reference and many of the methods and techniques for the study of voting behavior should have come from market analysis. Methods of sampling preferences among commodities, stocks, services, trade names, and so forth were applied to sampling actual or potential preferences in political campaigns, legislative assemblies, and even courts of law. It was natural that leading political pollsters, as they came to be known, should also be among the leading market analysts.

Voting behavior and decision-making

But the analogy between consumer preferences in the market and voting preferences at the polls proved, at best, to be a strained one, notwithstanding the effort by scholars like Anthony Downs to equate the two. We know, also, that factors involved in voting behavior at the polls are not identical with those that operate in legislative assemblies, administrative tribunals, or courts of law. Voting behavior in small groups is not identical with such behavior in large groups. Voting in presidential elections involves factors not similarly engaged in voting at state-wide or local elections. And there are significant differences in the decision-making process (i.e., voting) as it operates in a Committee of the Whole Congress, a standing committee, and a more specialized subcommittee. Thus political science has become increasingly preoccupied with research on the behavior of systems and subsystems of political power.

But voting behavior or decision-making as a frame of reference for the study of political science is no philosopher's stone. Its great value is to focus attention upon dynamic factors in the political process which political philosophers, historians, and lawyers have been inclined to take for granted, minimize or neglect. Because Behavioralism concerns itself with *acts* in a variety of political situations, it lends itself more readily than do other frames of reference to objective and quantitative methods of description and analysis. Because the behavioralist subordinates imagination to observation and metaphysical abstractions to "observed realities," he has carried political science another step in the direction of becoming what Auguste Comte hoped it might someday be—a positive science. Moreover, increasing skill in the use of quantitative methods has helped to improve the quality of both politics and administration as well as to strengthen the theoretical structure of political science as a scientific enterprise. The development of improved procedures for sampling, interviewing, and observing populations, and for the coding and analysis of data, have added new dimensions to nearly every aspect of political science. New data-processing equipment has speeded up the accumulation of knowledge concerning political behavior by a factor not easily estimated.

The problem of communication

Behavioralism, moreover, offers a frame of reference in terms of which political scientists, like sociologists, economists, anthropologists, historians, lawyers, philosophers, psychologists, and even humanists can communicate with one another. For, as Wesley Mitchell emphasized in 1939, "all the social sciences [and the humanities] are concerned with the same theme—human behavior." This opportunity for communication if not integration in terms of human behavior is no small thing.* We have learned, after a fashion, to live with the traditional division of human knowledge into the social sciences, the natural sciences, religion, fine arts, and the humanities. But we know that if anything that can be called civilization is to survive, these disciplines cannot live in isolation. It may well be the role of the social sciences, if not to close the gap between what C. P. Snow has called "the two cultures," then at least to mediate among

* *Eleven Twenty-Six*, ed. Louis Wirth (University of Chicago Press, 1940), p. 115.

them. But if social science is to do this and thus help maintain that measure of both order and freedom essential to any viable civilization, it must look to its own house.

The process of specialization which long ago separated natural from moral philosophy continued through the years to produce further fragmentation. Political economy broke away from moral philosophy, economics from political economy, political science from both economics and history. In a kind of intellectual fission the process of specialization went on unabated even within these disciplines themselves. In 1939 Wesley Mitchell, speaking at a Social Science Conference, said, "We are worried by symptoms of disintegration within the several social sciences." In economics he pointed to the proliferation of subspecialties including "mathematical theorists, econometrists, agricultural economists, and specialists in labor problems, money and banking, public finance, merchandising, business cycles . . . and various other subjects. Each set of specialists has knowledge the other sets do not possess and what each set publishes is becoming less intelligible to the other sets."

A similar trend has set in among political scientists, with specialists in public administration, public law, comparative government, political parties, pressure groups, public opinion, and legislation, developing methods and vocabularies which frustrate rather than facilitate communication. Even political theory and public policy have been specialized to a point where no one can say for sure what they mean. Even Behavioralism, which many hoped could serve as a new and common frame of reference, is in danger of becoming a cult preoccupied with the precise measurement of trivia or the demonstration of self-evident truths. What shall it profit us to be told with elaborate charts and tables, scattergrams and regression equations, that "opinions are really formed through the day-to-day exchange of observations and comments which goes on among people"? * Or in another seminal study of voting behavior that "the results . . . conform to the basic psychological principle that where strong and opposing forces act on an individual the resultant behavior will demonstrate the characteristics of conflict." † How far have we come and how much new knowledge do we acquire by learning after elaborate surveys and analyses that turnout at elections is a function of voter interest? ‡

* See Bernard Berelson, *et al.*, *Voting* (Chicago: University of Chicago, 1954).

† See Angus Campbell, *et al.*, *The Voter Decides* (Evanston: Row, Peterson & Co., 1954).

‡ See Angus Campbell, *et al.*, *The American Voter* (New York: John Wiley, 1960).

Psychology, sociology, and politics

A good deal of contemporary behavioral research by political scientists has produced results so obvious or so remote from the political process as to make them of doubtful value to the student of *political* behavior. As Professor V. O. Key has said, "The style set in the Erie County study of voting, *The People's Choice*, threatens to take the politics out of the study of electoral behavior." The fact is that psychology, or at least social psychology and sociology, has enveloped contemporary political science like a shroud. This in itself is not wholly to be deplored. The contributions of psychologists and sociologists to political science have been numerous and significant. Unfortunately, many political scientists, rejecting the contributions of political philosophers, historians, constitutional lawyers, and other students of both politics and administration, have abandoned politics for a kind of pseudo psychology and/or ersatz sociology.

To make use of relevant knowledge from these and other disciplines is altogether wise and necessary if a social science is to emerge from a wilderness of specialized social sciences. In all this there is nothing new. Aristotle levied upon what today would be called economics, history, philosophy, and even psychology in his lectures on politics. So did Hobbes and Locke and Hume, Mill and Bentham, Graham Wallas, A. V. Dicey, John Dewey, and, in our own generation, Charles Merriam, A. L. Lowell, and Harold Lasswell. But politics remained their central concern—not politics merely as a form of psychic release or abnormal behavior but as the management of the common affairs of the community for the common good of all. When political scientists *abandon* politics as the major focus of their research, they become poor political scientists without becoming much of anything else. Moreover, they abdicate a crown for a servant's cap—for it is to politics that men must look for that integrative process without which there can be neither order nor freedom.

The age of analysis

Specialization among and within the major disciplines has no doubt made possible the contemporary Knowledge Explosion. But we need to be aware of some of its implications. The age of science is an age of analysis, and analysis means "to unloose, to dissolve," . . . to separate "anything whether an object of the senses or of the intellect into constituent parts or elements." In nearly every branch of science analysis has succeeded in pulling our world apart. Reality has been reduced to smaller and smaller particles. The behavioral sciences have dissolved society and the state into cultures and subcultures, systems and subsystems, and these into classes, groups, or interests forever clashing in a kind of Hobbesian state of nature. Classes, groups, and interests, in their turn, have been reduced to smaller and smaller groups and micro-politics itself becomes a new field of specialization. At one point in the analysis individuals vanish altogether in the group or are seen only as psycho-political organisms, pushed this way and that by forces beyond their ken or their control, behaving to all intents and purposes strictly according to Newton's Second Law. Functionally the individual is replaced by the *role* or *roles* he is compelled by circumstances to play. Much of this is then either forgotten or mentioned only by reference, as individual behavior is attributed wholly to the influence of such factors as age, sex, social and economic status. In more recondite research these factors then are studied in a context of Freudian or Neo-Freudian analysis in which the influence of infantile sexuality and psychic traumas of various kinds are seen to operate within a personality straining for equilibrium among the forces of the Id, Super-Ego, and Ego.

Analysis of this kind has helped to make political

science, or the science of political behavior, more objective, empirical, and rational. But in the process political behavioralists, proud of their own rationality, have laid such emphasis on psycho-physical forces at work both in the person and in his political environment that the role of reason in the political process has had short shrift. The eighteenth-century model of the free rational citizen all but disappeared as political behavior was conceived to be essentially if not altogether non-rational and determined. "The empirical art of politics," wrote Graham Wallas, "consists largely in the creation of opinion by the deliberate exploitation of subconscious, nonrational inference." How far this is from Aristotle's notion that "the mind governs the appetite with a political or kingly power!" When reason *is* admitted at all in some contemporary behavioral research, it comes in only as a special kind of conditioned behavior essential in perception and analysis but not in the decision-making process. According to David Hume, a much-neglected behavioralist, "reason is and ought only to be the slave of the passions." Political behavior, in these terms, is, as Harold Lasswell has said, the nonrational projection of private affects upon public objects.

Toward integration and understanding

Analysis, I have said, means to dissolve—to disintegrate, not to integrate. The progressive disintegration of matter into smaller and smaller particles and of human behavior into smaller and smaller components poses a number of problems for both natural and social science. Among these is the gap between appearance and reality and the nature of reality itself. When the body of John Doe is reduced to its basic elements and placed in neatly labeled bottles on a laboratory shelf, one is driven to ask, what is the real John Doe? Is it in the bottles on the shelf or in the living, breathing, feeling, thinking, loving, hating, fearing guy we call John Doe? When the political community is reduced to a discontinuous series of systems and subsystems, groups, or interests, what happens to the community? When individual postmen, doctors, lawyers, teachers, or voters with distinctive names and personalities are reduced to impersonal roles like shadows in a cave or masks in a pageant, what happens to the individuals? Are the rights and privileges of free men attributes of real living men and women or of groups and systems or perhaps merely of roles? And in any case which are the real components of society and the state, of the systems and subsystems, of the groups or classes we talk so much about? Is it possible, without offense to the most rigorous canons of science, to restore the individual to the behavioral equation?

The Age of Analysis poses another problem—the establishment or re-establishment of order and meaning among otherwise disparate and meaningless elements. For analysis may clarify, but it does not as such create knowledge. Knowledge comes not from more and more information about less and less but from the facts of life seen in some meaningful context. Hence the effort of all scientists to conceptualize, to find concepts which will restore some unity and meaning to the fragments of reality their analysis has revealed. The process of conceptualization takes many forms. It appears in the effort to establish statistical uniformities or trends; to describe forms or types of individuals, roles or classes, groups, and interests; to classify various kinds of behavior, political systems, and even to outline norms, goals, standards, or values in terms of which behavior may be conditioned or guided. It is in the accumulation of these concepts and in their continuous testing and analysis that our knowledge expands.* Up to very recent modern

* See for example: Ferrel Heady and Sybil Stokes: *Papers in Comparative Administration* (University of Michigan, 1963), especially Chaps. I, II, and III, where the "Sala Model," "Infor-

times it is concepts derived from the philosophical, historical, legal, and administrative frames of reference that have furnished the main body of knowledge in political science. Power, the state, sovereignty, nation, monarchy, aristocracy, democracy, federalism, liberty, due process, feudalism, capitalism, socialism, communism, liberalism, conservatism, the public interest are but a few taken at random.

The fact-value syndrome

Political concepts of more recent times and especially those associated with a behavioral frame of reference strive mainly to describe and give meaning to what *is* or to what under certain circumstances *will* be. In general, contemporary behavioralists eschew concepts of what *ought* to be or even of what *could* be were people of a mind to have it so. It is in this sense that they are *value* free—believing that to confuse what *is* or is going to be with what *ought* or *could* be would impair

---

mation-Energy Model," and the "Bureaucratic Model" are considered.

See also as examples: "Models in a Behavioral Theory of the Firm," by R. M. Cyret and others; "The Logical Nature of an Action System," by M. Kochen and Marion Levy, Jr.; and "Communication Systems and Soviet Systems, A Statistical Exploration in History and Policy," by Daniel Lerner—all in *Behavioral Science,* vol. 4, Nos. 1 and 2, and vol. 2, No. 4.

their objectivity and import imagination and wishful thinking into what can otherwise be a positive science. To *be scientific,* they seem to say, one must be neutral among values, and indifferent to the outcome of the great game of politics.*

It is this posture, as much as anything, that accounts for the failure of the behavioral frame of reference to give new life and new direction to political science. It is this assumption that helps to explain the monumental accumulation of data and

* One may note in this connection, the article by Arthur Schlesinger, Jr., in the *New Statesman* for Feb. 8, 1963, in which he contrasts the Pragmatic and the Utopian liberal. The Utopian being the idealist who sees a vision of a good society without the will or the wit (practical means) to achieve it. The Pragmatist subordinates "ideals to results."

Or even more portentous are remarks by President Kennedy that political points of view, political problems are less and less important. "The fact of the matter is," he told an Economic Conference in Washington, May 21, 1962, "that most of the problems, or at least many of them, that we now face are technical problems, are administrative problems."

And later at Yale in 1962, he said, "What is at stake . . . today is not some grand warfare of rival ideologies . . . but the practical management of a modern economy. . . . Political labels and clichés are irrelevant."

This retreat from politics is to be noted also in such statements as the following by Seymour Lipsit: "Democracy," he says, "is not only or even primarily a means through which different groups can attain their ends or seek the good society, it is the good society itself in operation."

Does this mean, as Dr. Pangloss would have said, that "This *is* the best of all possible worlds. All we need now is to study the techniques of how to manage it."

See: "Politics of the Possible," by Stephen Rousseas and James Farganis, in *The Nation,* Mar. 23, 1963.

the meager crop of significant concepts. What pass for concepts are often little more than semantic neologisms, useless as scientific concepts and incomprehensible to everyone but their inventors. It is this neutrality or indifference to the outcome of current conflicts over values that tends to trivialize political science and make it a more or less sophisticated mechanism for the manipulation of human behavior—regardless of goal or purpose. A scientist without values is like a fanatic who redoubles his effort having lost his aim. I would argue that, unless science itself is merely random behavior without purpose or meaning, a not inconsiderable part of its purpose is to discover, develop, describe, and serve basic human needs.* I would argue further that this lays a special obligation on political science, for politics has become the major integrative process in all human societies.

* "In my opinion," says Galileo in Bertolt Brecht's play of that name, "the only goal of science is to alleviate the hardships of human existence. If men of science, intimidated by self-seeking rules, are content merely to store up knowledge for the sake of knowledge, science can be crippled and your new machines mean only new oppression. In time you may discover everything that can be discovered anl still your progress will be progress away from humanity. The distance between you and them can one day become so great that your joyous cry over some new gain could be answered by a universal shriek of horror. . . . As things are now, the most that one can hope for is a race of inventive pygmies that can be hired for anything."

See Jörn Donner, *Report from Berlin* (Bloomington: Indiana University Press, 1961), p. 117.

Behavioral science has no mandate to be indifferent to human goals or values. On the contrary, one of its major assumptions is that human behavior is goal-directed, and that in striving for these goals men choose among alternative modes of conduct or behavior. It assumes also that, in choosing, men are "conditioned" by a wide variety of factors in their psycho-political field or environment, including formal education in rational modes of thought and behavior. This conditioning may involve not only formal instruction by precept and example but also action to change those conditions that impair one's ability to make rational choices. Such rationally induced changes in the subject and his environment with corresponding changes in behavior will require the conscious manipulation of value symbols quite as much as the conscious manipulation of the physical environment.

Political science and manipulation

It is this aspect of modern behavioralism that has given rise to widespread criticism of those who practice these recondite if not occult arts. Skillful and cunning men, it is said, versed in the mysteries of psychological conditioning and armed with modern methods of communication may use these techniques to control human behavior for predetermined and selfish ends. No one familiar with modern advertising and the content of modern mass media can be indifferent to this danger. But behavioralists can also encourage conscious and rational reflection on the human condition and on alternative roads to those basic goals for which mankind strives.

Moreover, because modern behavioralism discounts innate ideas and assumes that environmental influences are paramount, it opens vast possibilities for the development of human character and personality through rationally induced changes in the physical environment and in human behavior as well.

Nor can political scientists be indifferent to what these changes are or can be. The Knowledge Explosion has brought a dramatic extension in man's life expectancy and a more abundant life to millions. It has at the same time produced a Population Explosion that may well reduce other millions to hunger if not starvation. Increased knowledge has increased human mobility. The world has become a neighborhood, and outer space a new frontier. But in the process we have multiplied space machines until our cities strangle in traffic and smother in smog. And the energy released by nuclear fission has produced a balance of terror among nations, as the world stands on a razor's edge of ultimate disintegration—the final awful fruit of an Age of Analysis.

Almost none of these and other problems that confront the human race can be solved by the natural sciences or by a social science indifferent to the fate of mankind. Nor can they be met by elaborate analyses of political power without regard for the purposes for which power is used. Continued preoccupation with methodology or with process and procedure to the neglect of policy or purpose may, in fact, be what one Harvard psychologist has called a "failure of nerve" in the social sciences, a kind of escapism in which techniques provide a refuge from the risky or dangerous political issues. I think it was Freud who once said, "There comes a time when you ought to stop cleaning your spectacles and take a look through them." This is not a plea for sloppy science or sentimentalism, but for a reorientation of political science at least toward goals more compatible with its great traditions than the accumulation of trivia and the ponderous elaboration of platitudes.

Part of our problem, of course, is that political science has been at best a starveling, a poor relation of technology and applied natural science. It has also suffered an *instrumental* poverty when compared with the natural sciences or even with psychology. What research tools do we have to compare with the microscope, telescope, thermometer, let alone the cyclotron, bevatron, synchrotron? *

Someday we shall come to see that research and training in the science and art of government are at least as important and as deserving of support as are researches in nuclear physics and chemistry. In a daring book called *Daedalus,* published nearly forty years ago, J. B. S. Haldane said: "I think that the tendency of applied science is to magnify injustices until they become too intolerable to be borne. . . . I think [also]," he said, "that moral progress is so difficult that any developments are to be welcomed which present it [i.e., moral progress] as the naked alternative to destruction, no matter how horrible may be the stimulus which is neces-

* Lacking the precise instruments of the natural sciences and the advantages of the controlled experiment, political scientists have turned to model building, simulation and games theory to test relevant political concepts. When this type of analysis can itself be tested against political behavior in the real world, it can be a useful and creative instrument. Otherwise, however much fun it may be and however much it may sharpen men's wits, it is of dubious scientific value. Referring to some of the war-simulations now carried on by social scientists a recent critic has said, "What is remarkable to me is that the scientific and engineering communities . . . have displayed such blindness in their acceptance of the . . . scientific claims of war-simulation games—claims so unsupported by even the most rudimentary scientific controls as to belong in the class of the electric healing belt and seaweed tonics that restore vitality." See Herbert Schenck, Jr., of M.I.T., in *The Nation,* June 15, 1963.

sary before men will take the moral step in question."

Have we now reached that point in history where the alternatives to moral and political progress are so horrible that we may at long last be willing to put forth the effort necessary to control and guide political power as we are learning to control and guide nuclear power? Unless we do so, we shall surely die.

It is in that area where conscience and power meet that political science must make its greatest contribution. In the present state of nature which characterizes the relations among nations, power alone now has the floor and the still, small voice of conscience is scarcely heard. Life in such a state is bound to be solitary, nasty, brutish, and short. "Never," said President Kennedy to the United Nations Assembly, "have the nations of the world had so much to lose and so much to gain. Together we shall save our planet or together we shall perish in its flames. Save it we can. Save it we must."

This is the task to which political science, without delay, must dedicate itself. For it remains true today, as it was in Plato's time, that "the greatest and fairest sort of wisdom is concerned with the ordering of states."

III

Use and abuse of political power

"Power," said Lord Acton in a much-quoted phrase, "tends to corrupt and absolute power corrupts absolutely." It is with this proposition that we are now concerned. As a political scientist, I have a special concern in Lord Acton's grim comment—for the scientific study of politics has as its central core the study of political power. It would be easy to say simply that power itself does not corrupt although it may be used for corrupt or ignoble ends. Few, I suppose, would deny that where power is used to limit or to enslave the human spirit it does, in fact, corrupt both those who exercise it and their victims. One thinks of the long recital of such abuses in the Old Testament, one thinks of the siege of Troy and the slaughter of its inhabitants, of the urbane and highly civilized government of ancient Athens condemning Socrates to death and of the trial and crucifixion of Jesus. And in more recent times one thinks of the abuse of public power in the service of racial, religious, and political persecution and of the monumental abuse of power in the innumerable wars among nations, creeds, and classes which have brought death and desolation to millions in nearly every country and continent in the world. Attila the Hun, Napoleon Bonaparte, Mussolini, Adolf Hitler, Josef Stalin—these are but a few names on an almost endless roster of men whose abuse of power has become legendary. Surely you might say with Lord Acton, "power corrupts."

But there is another side to the coin where power does not enslave but liberates, does not destroy but builds. One thinks of the use of power in ancient times to create the glorious culture of Periclean Athens and the grandeur that was Rome. One thinks of public schools and highways, hospitals and playgrounds, and all manner of public services made possible only by the use of public power. One thinks of Jefferson and the Declaration of Independence, of Washington and the establishment of our constitutional system, of Lincoln and the Emancipation Proclamation, and of many others who have used power wisely and well. All of this you know without my saying so. But I should like to take a somewhat different and closer look at this thing we call power—and how in cases where the issues are not so clear we can distinguish between the proper use and the abuse of power.

The nature of political power

We must understand that power comes in many forms and sizes. We speak of the horsepower of an automobile or a steam locomotive. We speak of economic power, the power of the press and of public opinion, of power systems, power elites, and so on. Yet in all its various uses the term has a fairly constant and consistent meaning. I am told by classical scholars that its roots are to be found in Greek words meaning both "to start" and "to rule" or to control. In his book on *Metaphysics,* Aristotle explained that a powerful individual or group is one "at whose will that which is moved is moved and that which changes, changes." Power, someone has said, is what makes things go, wheels to turn, ships to sail, men to move in particular ways. Power is the great initiator, the cosmic self-starter that starts everything else and keeps it going.*

Although power has become a common term in the natural sciences, its earliest, most continuous, and consistent usage has been in political science. When Aristotle in the *Metaphysics* sought for illustrations of power, he cited "magistrates in cities, oligarchs, monarchs and tyrants." When we loosely refer to the power of the sun or the sea or an earthquake—or the power of a motor or a locomotive—what we probably mean is not power in the classical sense but "energy." † Energy can become power only when it is harnessed, guided, and controlled. For, as Bertrand Russell has said, power implies "the production of intended effects." ‡

The energy of falling water becomes power when it is channeled and controlled to drive an electric generator. Energy uncontrolled as in a typhoon or a storm at sea, or in a motorcar whose steering apparatus is gone, can be dangerous and destructive. We say it is out of control or in a technical sense has not been transformed into power.

* See "Power and Violence," by E. V. Walter in *American Political Science Review*, June, 1964.

† See Romano Guardini, *Power and Responsibility* (Chicago: Regnery, 1961).

‡ See Russell, *Power: A New Social Analysis* (London: 1962), p. 25.

But power, too, can be dangerous and destructive where energies are directed toward dangerous and destructive ends. And it is, I suppose, because political power may be abused that Lord Acton said that "power tends to corrupt and absolute power corrupts absolutely." But this aphorism tends to emphasize the negative or destructive possibilities of power and to overlook its use for creative, constructive, liberating ends.

In its most general sense power in human affairs involves the control of human behavior for particular ends through the express or implied threat of punishment for those who refuse or fail to comply. Power, of course, is not the only means of controlling human behavior. Influence through education and indoctrination may be equally, or even more, effective. Power differs from influence mainly in that it involves the actual or potential application of penalties of some kind to those whose behavior deviates from what is required. Thus we may say that power is the ability to make and *enforce* decisions (i.e., laws, decrees, rules, or regulations) affecting particular patterns of human behavior. Without the ability to *enforce* decisions we cannot speak of power or for that matter of government, for government is simply the making and *enforcing* of decisions concerning certain kinds of behavior. To *enforce* decisions means in final analysis the application of penalties upon those who fail to comply.

Power structures—power elites

In this general sense, power is widely diffused in nearly every society and can be found in virtually every kind of organized group activity, from the government of the United States to that of the P.T.A. Corporations, trade unions, colleges and universities, even churches and families, have their governing boards or officials, who in one way or another make and enforce decisions concerning the behavior of their members. Those who govern in all of these various organized groups make up what is called the power structure or the power elites of society. As one looks at the total picture one is reminded of the familiar rhyme—

> *There never was a tiny flea but had a flea to bite him*
> *And on that flea another flea and so ad infinitum.*

Like the pecking order of the barnyard, there seems to be a pecking or power order among human beings. Small wonder that Aristotle called man a political animal, which, I suppose, is another way of calling him a power-seeking animal. Indeed, Thomas Hobbes, the greatest of English political philosophers, observing that the quest for power among men seemed so universal, placed it at the very top of man's value system. "I put [in the first place]," he said, "a general inclination of all mankind, a perpetual and restless desire of Power after Power that ceaseth only in death." Some contemporary psychologists have even suggested that this continuous and virtually universal quest for power may in fact be a major factor in mental health. Karen Horney, for example, says that a "striving for power serves as a protection against [a sense of] helplessness which . . . is one of the basic elements of anxiety." The more one feels frustrated and helpless the more does one wish to avoid the appearance of weakness or inadequacy—and, as Karen Horney says, "a striving for power serves as a protection against the danger of feeling or being regarded as insignificant." *

To avoid these dangers one strives either for power or for identification with power elites—a process which in the family may result in a father fixation or deification. In the political world it may help to explain the appeal of strong charismatic leaders to millions of voters who see them as father images or power symbols.

* Karen Horney, *The Neurotic Personality of Our Time* (New York: Norton, 1937), p. 166. Also see Patrick Mullahy, *Oedipus: Myth and Complex* (New York: Hermitage, 1948), p. 67.

However universal the distribution or the striving for power may be, one must note that all power structures are not the same nor are all power elites equal. Some, to quote George Orwell, are more equal than others, although recent efforts by political scientists to measure various increments of power and influence have not been conspicuously successful.* A crude measure would be the number of people whose behavior is affected by decisions that are made and enforced in the process of government. The power elite in any system, according to the late C. Wright Mills, "is composed of men whose positions enable them to . . . make decisions having *major* consequences"—that is, affecting large populations.†

Power structures or systems are usually hierarchical in form with those at the top normally having more power than those at lower levels since decisions made and enforced at the top of the pyramid have more widespread effect than those

* See, for example, L. S. Shapley and Martin Shubik, "A Method of Evaluating the Distribution of Power in a Committee System," *American Political Science Review*, Vol. 48 (1954); James G. March, "Measurement Concepts in the Theory of Influence," *Journal of Politics*, Vol. 19 (1957); also James G. March, "An Introduction to the Theory of Measurement of Influence," *American Political Science Review*, Vol. 49 (1955); William H. Riker, "Some Ambiguities in the Notion of Power," *American Political Science Review*, Vol. 58 (June, 1964).

† C. W. Mills, *The Power Elite* (New York: Oxford, 1956), p. 4.

made farther down. Hence, a person's position in the hierarchy is a crude measure of his power and prestige within the system. The president of a local P.T.A. may reasonably be described as having less power and prestige than the President of the United States and, consequently, he is less able to use it for good or evil ends.*

Public and private power systems

It is important to recognize the variety and complexity of the power systems that one finds in a modern industrial society. Thus far we have lumped the governments of corporations, trade unions, churches, schools and colleges, and even families, together with federal, state and local governments as parts of the total power structure in

* It would, however, be too much to say that any particular person's power can be exactly measured by his position in any particular power system. A classroom teacher of great energy and zeal may in fact exercise more power—i.e., affect the behavior of more people—than a lazy, indifferent superintendent of schools. And there are many subordinate officials in the vast federal bureaucracy whose actual power exceeds that of those who outrank them. The chairman of an important congressional committee may be more powerful in the decision-making process than a majority of his colleagues or the President himself. Nevertheless, I think it is reasonable to say that those at the top of any power structure have more power than those down the line. This, perhaps, accounts for the fact that the intensity and significance of the power struggle in any organization is likely to increase as one moves from lower to higher levels of rank and status.

the United States. But there are significant differences between those which may be described as private governments; i.e., corporations, trade unions, etc., and those described as public governments. Public power systems claim jurisdiction over all persons who reside in a given territory. No one residing in the territory of a public government can escape its jurisdiction. The major exceptions to this are the representatives of foreign nations who by international law or courtesy enjoy a limited immunity from the power of the country in which they temporarily reside. For all other persons living within its territorial limits the jurisdiction of a public power system is compulsory. This is not true of private power systems. Members of trade unions, churches, colleges, corporations, may escape their jurisdiction by resignation, secession, divorce, or by selling their stock or other interest in the organization. But a man, or for that matter any private government, living outside the jurisdiction of any public power system is very rare indeed.

An equally important difference between public and private power systems is to be found in the kind of penalties by which their decisions may be enforced. Members of trade unions who break the rules of the union may be fined, suspended, or even expelled. Employees of corporations, members of churches, and other such private governments may also be fined, suspended, dismissed, or otherwise disciplined when they disobey or defy the decisions made by the organization. But in none of these may they be legitimately punished by imprisonment or death. Only public governments can *legitimately* use physical coercion to enforce their decisions—i.e., their laws, rules, or regulations.* It is this claim to compulsory jurisdiction over all persons living in a given territory and this monopoly of physical coercion that, in final analysis, distinguish public from private power systems. As John Locke put the matter, "*political* power is the right of making laws with penalties of death and consequently all less penalties for regulating and preserving property and of employing the force of the community in the execution of such laws." †

The compulsory jurisdiction of public governments and their monopoly of all legitimate coercive power makes their control of transcendent importance—for it is upon them that the peace, security, and freedom of all men depend. Only when individuals and private governments are

* Perhaps one should note as an exception the so-called corporal punishment often meted out by teachers and parents to children who disobey. But in most civilized communities even this exception is becoming less and less frequent as corporal punishment is increasingly frowned upon or forbidden by law.

† Locke: *The Second Treatise of Civil Government* (New York: Macmillan, 1947), p. 122.

willing to give up the private exercise of force and violence can we speak realistically of that "law and order" upon which civilization depends. And one may add that only when public governments now organized as sovereign nation-states are willing to give up their own monopoly of force in a larger community of nations can we hope for that *Perpetual Peace* of which Immanuel Kant and others have dreamed.

Power and influence—coercion and consent

Because political power carries with it the threat of force against those who fail to comply with the decisions that are made, the symbols of power are often the sword and the shield or, in modern usage, the guided missile or the atomic bomb. It is for this reason, I suppose, that we sing of the "Army and Navy Forever—Three Cheers for the Red, White and Blue." But the *use* of force, even in primitive societies, is an exception. More often than not it is influence rather than force or the threat of force that makes people law abiding. *Persuasion* is not only more common than the use or threat of force but more effective. That is why the English political philosopher Thomas Hill Green argued that it is *will*, or consent, not forced compliance, that is the most enduring basis for political power.*

It is this underlying *will,* or *consensus,* that makes any government or power system *legitimate* by investing it with *authority*. Without authority, political power lies exposed as naked force—an unstable basis for government of any kind. Where authority is lacking, the transfer of power from one ruler or one party to another is almost invariably accompanied by force and violence. Hence a central goal of every power system is to invest it with *authority*—i.e., to make it legitimate. This is accomplished by a complex process of political socialization involving education and indoctrination through the family, schools, churches, and other voluntary groups, political parties, pressure groups, and all major channels of mass communication. Important in this process also are charismatic leadership and political symbolism. A George Washington, a Queen Elizabeth can contribute significantly to this end. Nor should we think of the flag, the mace and scepter, the orb and the crown, as childish baubles of kings and potentates. On the contrary, they are symbols of the "power and glory" of the state which sheath the naked sword of power

* One is reminded of Talleyrand's advice to Napoleon that "You can do many things with bayonets except to sit comfortably enthroned upon them."

with authority and make compliance, if not pleasant, at least palatable.

To invest power with authority or legitimacy, however, does not put an end to political conflict. Within the framework of legitimate authority, conflict continues over *who* shall govern, *how*, and *for what* ends. In stable political systems this conflict resolves itself essentially into a peaceful conflict over the authoritative allocation of values—values which have been summarized by Harold Lasswell as income, deference, and safety. Politics in this sense involves a continuous struggle among individuals, factions, interest groups (sometimes called pressure groups), and political parties—to influence or control political power for certain ends. The nature of this struggle and of the contending forces involved depends in large measure upon the political system and the composition and values of the society within which the struggle takes place.

Constitutional limitations on power

Much will depend upon the political system, whether it be parliamentary or presidential, unitary or federal. Is the system based on universal suffrage or more restricted participation? Is there a one-party, two-party, or multi-party system? What about the system of representation and election? Is it based on single or multiple member districts, on majority vote or proportional representation? Even the form of the ballot—whether it be secret or open, party column or office block—can affect the political struggle. Not least are the constitutional limitations imposed upon the exercise of political power as in our own Constitution and Bill of Rights, all designed to prevent an abuse of power. Freedom of speech and press and the rights of free assembly and of religious worship are guaranteed against impairment by public authorities not only because they are essential to the engineering of consent but as good in themselves. Slavery and involuntary servitude, except as a punishment for crime, are forbidden. So, too, are arbitrary arrest, illegal search and seizure, and self-incrimination. Every exercise of power must assure the individual of due process, including the right to counsel in criminal cases, a fair hearing before an impartial jury, and equal protection of the law. Power is further limited by the allocation of authority between the central government and the state and among the branches of the government itself—executive, legislative, and judicial. In this way, as James Madison observed, "ambition is made to counteract ambition," to prevent the abuse of public power.

At the other end of the scale are the totalitarians, whether Fascists or Communists, who identify the political state with society and extend coercive political power to every facet of human life. To be sure, the Communists defend the totalitarian state only as a temporary expedient—as a necessary device of the proletariat for liquidating class conflict, transforming society, and reconditioning human nature. Ultimately, they profess to believe, the state will wither away to be replaced by a cooperative, communistic commonwealth. Thus anarchism and communism converge on the plane of philosophical speculation. In the meantime, however, the political state does not wither away. Private property, mines, factories and farms, homes, churches, schools and colleges remain in its possession and education, religion, cultural and even domestic affairs are subject to strict surveillance and control by those vested with coercive power. The operational code of present-day totalitarians was succinctly expressed by the late Italian Fascist, Mussolini: "Nothing outside the State—Nothing against the State—Everything within the State."

The middle way—liberalism and conservatism

Between the two extremes of anarchism and totalitarian communism or fascism are to be found other political ideologies committed in varying degrees to the use of political power for social ends. Among them are classical liberalism, conservatism, and social democracy or, as it is often called, utopian or democratic socialism. Classical liberals like Adam Smith, J. S. Mill, Thomas Macaulay, and Herbert Spencer attacked virtually all forms of public intervention in social and economic affairs. Such intervention they believed to be an abuse of power. "Political means to achieve social ends," said Macaulay, "will destroy (both) liberty and prosperity if not civilization itself." To Herbert Spencer the public regulation of economic activity and most welfare legislation were signs of a coming slavery. "Laissez faire!" they cried—leave things alone. Competition in a free market for ideas and for goods and services is the best guarantee of freedom and prosperity.

Conservatives, on the other hand, in their devotion to established authority extolled the intervention of the political state, especially to protect private property and status. In England, conservative doctrine included spirited defense of the monarchy, an established church, a hereditary aristocracy, colonialism, and a centralized imperial authority. Although opposed to state-sponsored welfare programs, they were not opposed to the use of public power to protect vested property rights through protective tariffs, public subsidies, and other favors of this kind.

Social Democrats or Democratic Socialists also extolled the intervention of public authority, not for the protection of private property and status but to promote social welfare. To this end they urged government ownership and operation of major industries and business establishments. Unlike the Communists, however, Social Democrats staunchly defended freedom of speech, press, religious worship, and other features of a democratic society against the coercive power of the political state.

This overly simplified summary of major political theories concerning the use and abuse of power needs extensive revision. The laissez faire liberalism of the eighteenth and early nineteenth centuries has become the welfare liberalism of today, a blood brother to democratic or utopian socialism. While English conservatives have come to embrace what Herbert Spencer once denounced as the "new Toryism" of a welfare state, American conservatism is torn between those who accept moderate welfare programs and the anti-welfare political philosophy of Herbert Hoover and Senator Goldwater. Social democracy or democratic socialism having seen many of its goals won under liberal or progressive banners seems to be losing faith in some of its traditional doctrines. Although government ownership of basic resources and industry is still proclaimed as a major goal, recent years have seen a retreat even from this.

The liberal tradition

In these shifting, ideological sands it is dangerous to generalize concerning contemporary doctrines on the use and abuse of political power. Closer analysis, however, will show considerable doctrinal consistency in those who carry on this great debate. The modern liberal no longer speaks of laissez faire but looks favorably upon state intervention especially where it is designed to remove inequality and to protect liberty. He remains basically libertarian in point of view with an often romantic faith in human nature and human perfectibility. He is opposed to state intervention to protect men from their own folly or from dangerous or immoral ideas and consequently is hostile to official censorship. He still believes with John Stuart Mill that "the sole end for which mankind are warranted, individually and collectively, in interfering with the liberty of action of any of their members is self-protection. . . . His own good, either physical or moral, is not sufficient warrant." The contemporary liberal, however, finds in this sufficient warrant for all manner of social and welfare legislation—not to reform individuals or to protect them from their own weakness or folly—but to safeguard others and to ensure a fair chance in a fair field for everyone.

Viewed in this light, liberalism has been more consistent than it may appear when one looks at its retreat from the laissez faire doctrines of Adam Smith and Herbert Spencer to those of the welfare state. Some fifty years ago L. T. Hobhouse published a volume on *Liberalism* which even today affords a fair summary of its central principles and goals. Liberals, he said, believe in civil liberty including universal suffrage and representative and responsible government at every level. Civil liberty also includes equal justice under law with all the procedural safeguards of the Bill of Rights and the abolition of special privileges based on class, race, color, or creed. Liberals believe, also, in what they call *fiscal liberty,* which they define as taxation according to ability to pay—or equality of sacrifice.

Personal liberty, including freedom of thought and expression, freedom of association for peaceful ends, religious liberty, and personal privacy, is among the central tenets of both classical and contemporary liberalism. But these, the liberal believes, are not enough to ensure what he calls *social liberty and equality,* which include political and legal equality for women, equality of opportunity for education, recreation, cultural enjoyment and enrichment, access to decent housing, medical care, and security in old age. To secure these, he believes, is a major responsibility of the political community and hence a proper use for political power. The contemporary liberal also believes in *economic liberty*. He is opposed to trusts and monopolies that impair free competition and is in favor of government regulation or ownership where this is necessary to protect the consumer from exploitation and the individual entrepreneur from unfair competition. The modern liberal continues to oppose protective tariffs and other political restraints on free trade and he believes in freedom of contract, including the right of labor to organize so that it may contract with employers on an equal footing. Liberals continue to favor self-determination for all peoples living under alien rule and are opposed to imperialism and colonialism. They also believe in decentralized decision-making whenever possible with all that this means in terms of local and regional self-government. Liberals, then as now, oppose war as an instrument of policy and favor disarmament and international cooperation to maintain peace and freedom. "In proportion as the world becomes free," they say, "the use of force becomes meaningless."

Although the environment of liberalism has

changed since Spencer wrote, its basic frame of reference and its underlying principles remain essentially the same.

Conservatism and conservatives—from Burke to Goldwater

What about conservatism and conservatives? Here, too, one can discern a fairly clear and consistent line from Edmund Burke to Barry Goldwater, but with important deviations here and there. If the central focus of liberalism is on liberty and equality—that of conservatism continues to be on order, property, and status. Conservatives and liberals differ not in their basic political values so much as in the order of priority which they assign to these values and the means for their realization. Both value order and liberty, but with a quite different rank order and a somewhat different meaning. When the liberal talks of liberty, he refers mainly to persons—when the conservative talks of liberty, he is more likely to refer not to persons but to property.* The liberal is suspicious of political

* Although this generalization is true in the main—one should also note that many constitutional conservatives are among the most fervent defenders of civil rights and personal freedom. One thinks in this connection, for example, of Charles Evans Hughes, William Howard Taft, and even the late Senator Robert Taft.

power, except as it is used to promote liberty and equality; the conservative is suspicious of public power, except as it is used to maintain order and protect property and status.

For a statement of the conservative position I turn again to an English writer, Lord Hugh Cecil, whose book on *Conservatism* first appeared in February, 1912. Political conservatism as a self-conscious ideology he traces to Edmund Burke. Burke, according to Lord Cecil, "insisted on the importance of religion and the value of its recognition by the State. Secondly he hated . . . with all his heart injustice to individuals committed in the course [or name] of political or social reform. Thirdly, he attacked the revolutionary conception of equality, and maintained the reality and necessity of distinctions of rank and station. Fourthly, he upheld private property as an institution sacred in itself and vital to the well-being of society. Fifthly, he regarded human society rather as an organism than a mechanism, and an organism about which there is much that is mysterious. Sixthly, . . . he urged the necessity of . . . continuity with the past and making changes as gradually and with as slight a dislocation as possible." *

Without pushing the point, these principles remain in large measure the core of American con-

* From *Conservatism* (New York: Henry Holt, 1912), p. 48.

servatism in 1965 as of English conservatism in 1912. While few contemporary conservatives would agree with Burke's defense of an established church, most of them would share his belief in religion as an important influence not only for human salvation but for maintaining public order. So, too, I believe, most contemporary conservatives would agree with Burke on the sanctity of private property. "I hope," said Burke, "that we shall never be so . . . lost to all sense of . . . social union, as, upon any pretext of public service, to confiscate the goods of a single unoffending citizen. Who but a tyrant . . . could think of seizing on the property of men . . . who that has not lost every trace of humanity, could think of casting down men of exalted rank . . . wherein they were maintained by their own landed property, [casting them down] to a state of indigence, depression and contempt." *

Few contemporary conservatives would fully share Burke's respect for the eighteenth-century system of rank and status. But, I suspect, many if not most of them *would* share his admiration for "the spirit of a gentleman," for that "mixed system of opinion and sentiment [which] had its origin in the ancient chivalry." † For conservatism, then as now, lays emphasis upon a certain "style of life

* *Ibid.*, p. 53.
† *Ibid.*, p. 55.

and conduct" on what Burke called "all the decent drapery of life * . . . [the] system of manners in every nation which a well formed mind would be disposed to relish." † By the same token the conservative today, as then, is deeply moved by time and tradition, by hallowed custom and ritual. Even our liberties, he believes, as did Burke, are an "entailed inheritance derived to us from our forefathers—to be transmitted to our posterity." ‡ With only a slight change in terms, most contemporary conservatives would say with Burke, "We have an inheritable crown; an inheritable peerage, and a House of Commons and a people inheriting privileges, franchises and liberties from a long line of ancestors." § Substitute our Constitution for Crown, our first families or contemporary elites for "peerage," and Congress for House of Commons, and this statement would not be out of place in the mouth of Russell Kirk or Barry Goldwater.

The conservative does not rule out change—but he would temper it with time and caution. "I would not exclude alteration," said Burke, "but even when I changed, it should be to preserve," || to preserve society and the state which, to the con-

* *Ibid.*, p. 56.
† *Ibid.*, p. 57.
‡ *Ibid.*, p. 58.
§ *Ibid.*, p. 58.
|| *Ibid.*, p. 60.

servative, are the real bearers of human values, the individual being but a kind of residuary legatee. "The individual," says Lord Cecil, "is largely the creation of the State. . . . It is the State and what depends on the State that makes the difference between civilisation and savagery." * But the conservative stops short at the intervention of the state for purposes that he believes are more properly left to the individual or the voluntary groups that we have called private governments. The coercive power of the state may be used to relieve widespread suffering not only in time of flood or famine but even in normal times as under the Elizabethan Poor Laws. In such cases, however, maximum reliance should be placed on private charity, the church, and other eleemosynary and philanthropic institutions. "No one," says Lord Cecil, "ought to be supported by the State in idleness." Even poor relief, he says, "may be justified [not as a matter of right or justice but] more simply as being expedient, and therefore on the same footing as national defense or any other kind of public expenditure," † to maintain public order. Poor relief is thus justified as a prudential safeguard against disorder and rebellion.

One may compare in this respect Senator Gold-

* *Ibid.*, p. 159.
† *Ibid.*, p. 177.

water's *Conscience of a Conservative.* "Let welfare," he says, "be a private concern. Let it be promoted by individuals and families, by churches, private hospitals, religious service organizations . . . that have been established for this purpose." * Otherwise, he says, we dehumanize such policies "by reducing charity to a mechanical operation." Making welfare a private responsibility, says Senator Goldwater, "is conducive to the spiritual as well as the material well-being of our citizens—and in a way that will preserve their freedom." Finally, as Burke and Lord Cecil would have said, if "public intervention is necessary, let the job be done by local and state authorities."

As for taxes—conservatives are as fearful of levies on income as on property. Any device "to regulate the amount of wealth which an individual may . . . acquire [and use]" is unjust. Hence, progressive income taxes and estate taxes are viewed with alarm. As Senator Goldwater says, "One problem with regard to taxes, then, is to enforce justice—to abolish the graduated features of our tax laws; and the sooner we get at the job the better." † But best of all is to reduce the volume of taxes by cutting public expenditures for education, health, and welfare. As soon as possible government should be re-

* Shepherdsville, Ky.: Victor Publishing Co., 1960, p. 74.
† *Ibid.*, p. 62.

duced to its *legitimate* functions of maintaining internal order, keeping foreign foes at bay, administering justice, and removing obstacles to the free interchange of goods. The exercise of these powers, says Senator Goldwater, "makes it possible for men to follow their chosen pursuits with maximum freedom." *

Notwithstanding conservative opposition to state intervention in economic and social affairs, and notwithstanding Senator Goldwater's plea for removal of obstacles to the free interchange of goods—conservative doctrine has not been generally opposed to tariffs, trade and shipping subsidies, and vast expenditures for national defense. In modern times at least, theirs has been a highly pragmatic or practical posture toward those policies which are designed to promote the economic and political power, independence, and glory of the national state.

Centralization vs. decentralization

If the major argument concerning the use and abuse of political power has focused on the question of state intervention in the social and economic life of the nation, there are other issues that ought not to be neglected. Among these are (1) the

* *Ibid.*, p. 17.

centralization or decentralization of political power and (2) the problem of international relations and organization. These issues cannot, of course, be disentangled completely from those which concern the intervention or nonintervention of public authority in the economic and social life of the community. Not infrequently those who cry out most loudly against centralization in public government are quite complacent about centralization in private government. The issue in many cases is, in fact, not one of centralization or decentralization but of public versus private government as the appropriate instrument. Thus the most strident critics of *federal* programs of economic regulation and welfare are often the same as those who oppose such programs at local, state, or regional levels. Slogans like "States' Rights" and "Local Self-Government" or "Federal Usurpation" are not infrequently used simply to conceal campaigns of opposition to the substance of particular public policies. Nevertheless, conflicts over particular policies are not unrelated to the assumption that human freedom and welfare will be most secure under a system based on the greatest possible decentralization of decision-making. In most cases, it is argued, this means, in a descending order of preference, the individual, a private government, local government, state government, federal government, or world government. The American bias for decentralization was expressed most eloquently by Alexis de Tocqueville. "Municipal institutions," he wrote, "constitute the strength of free nations. Town meetings are to liberty what primary schools are to science: they bring it within the people's reach, they teach men how to use and how to enjoy it." Unfortunately de Tocqueville's model had a closer fit to the pioneer agrarian society iof 1832, when he wrote, than to the highly integrated and mobile society of 1965.

For example, should contemporary decisions affecting the quality of food and drugs sold in commercial channels be left to the individual, the local community, the state or the nation? What about decisions affecting transportation and communication, or water supply, sanitation, stream and air pollution, the conservation, use, and management of natural resources, domestic relations, education, health, recreation, police and fire protection? There is, of course, no easy formula for answering such questions, and they continue to multiply as our society grows in size and complexity. A rapidly expanding population increasing in density and mobility generates new problems of government, new questions concerning the use and abuse of political power. Increasing specialization and a progressive division of labor increase interdependence not only among individuals but among industrial, business, labor, professional, and virtually all private groups, as well as local, state, regional, and national governments. Scientific and technological achievements affecting transportation and communication and the production and distribution of goods and services have increased the size and scope of corporate operations and have also revolutionized labor relations. Decisions affecting tens of millions of people in every part of the country are now made by corporation directors and labor leaders sitting in New York or Chicago or Detroit. Taken together all of these demographic and technical trends point to two seemingly irreversible political trends—the expansion of the role and functions of public governments, and increasing centralization of the decision-making process. The same forces are at work to transform problems of international relations and international organization.

Under the impact of supersonic travel, instantaneous communication, and international interdependence, national isolation or autarchy has become increasingly impossible. No man and no nation is an island any more. Any discussion concerning the use or abuse of power in trade and commerce, immigration, civil rights, cultural relations, and even national defense must take account of this new world or be condemned to blindness and futility. As we listen to the dialogue between liberals and conservatives, Socialists and Communists, we must continually ask how close they come to the realities of contemporary life. In the United States, since neither Fascists nor Communists have "cut much ice" in the argument over the use and abuse of power, we might look briefly at how our liberals and conservatives meet this test. We are, I believe, confronted at once with what may be called a Liberal Paradox and a Conservative Dilemma.

The liberal paradox and the conservative dilemma

The *liberal paradox* arises from the transition of liberal doctrine from nineteenth-century nationalism and laissez faire to late twentieth-century internationalism and the welfare state. We have seen how this transition has, in fact, been accomplished without any serious compromise of basic liberal doctrine as outlined by L. T. Hobhouse fifty years ago. The *conservative dilemma* is more pronounced in this country than in England where conservatives have with reasonable success moved from Edmund Burke to Disraeli and Winston Churchill—from devotion to throne and altar, order and status, to increasing dedication to a rapidly emerging welfare state and from nationalism and colonialism to the United Nations. If American conservatives continue to resist the powerful—some would say irresistible—thrust toward increasing intervention of public authority in the social and economic life of the nation, and increasing centralization of the decision-making process including some form of world organization, they will continue to lose touch with the real world and, I believe, cannot hope for an early return to power. So long as conservatives continue to regard these trends as an abuse of power, they will find themselves outside the mainstream not only of political thought in the world but of the underlying social forces to which political thought must adapt or die. For power itself does not corrupt save as it is used for corrupt and ignoble ends or for policies that fly in the face of reality and seek to impose the political world of 1865 on the scientific and technological world of 1965.

The use and abuse of power—some Constitutional Canons

May I, then, as a kind of coda to my main theme suggest some canons to guide our thinking about the use and abuse of power in the United States?

The Preamble to the Constitution sets forth the basic goals and purposes for which the coercive power of public authority may be used. In considering any particular public policy, therefore, we might ask ourselves whether or not it contributes to the realization of one or more of these goals. Does it help to promote a more perfect union, or to establish justice or provide for the common defense, or promote the general welfare and ensure liberty to ourselves and our posterity? And does it contribute to these ends not only at home but in our relations with other nations of the world?

The Constitution, as amended, outlines the means by which the goals and purposes of the Preamble are to be pursued. These include not only the instruments of government itself—Congress, the President, the Supreme Court, and the federal system—but the powers which they may legitimately use. The central government, for example, may regulate commerce, lay and collect taxes, borrow money, raise armies, provide for a navy, and so forth. All other powers are left to the people or to the states. The Constitution also imposes limitations upon public authorities in order to protect personal and private rights. We need to ask, then, of any particular exercise of public power, does it conform to some reasonable interpretation of these terms?

In deciding questions of this kind we might ask

also—do the policies proposed or adopted represent a reasonable response to the basic social, scientific, and technological forces at work here and abroad? If they do they can help to guide these forces to a realization of the goals outlined in the Preamble not as some utopian dream but as a rational response to the real world as it moves and changes from day to day. If they do not take account of this real world, they can at best serve as rationalizations of outmoded patterns of behavior or as futile protests against forces which we may not approve but which we cannot control.

Public opinion and public power

Finally, we need to ask whether public opinion as expressed at the polls, where it counts, will veto or sustain the policies made or proposed? In a democratic system all power is held subject to the ultimate consent of the governed, and this is as true of private as of public governments. In a democratic society the governments of corporations and trade unions, no less than federal, state and local governments, that fail to win the approval of the constituencies to which they are responsible—will be inherently unstable and ultimately impotent. To win this consent does not require power elites to defer decisions until the latest public opinion polls are recorded nor to slavishly acquiesce in every wave of popular prejudice or superstition. But it does require courageous and farseeing leadership not only in the decision-making process but in the continuous education of the voters upon whom these elites ultimately depend for whatever legitimate power and authority they have. Controversy and conflict over the use and abuse of power are at the heart of the political process. In stable but dynamic political systems controversies concerning the use or abuse of power will move continuously from conflict to consensus. In final analysis, if the decisions made and enforced are to be rational and viable they must represent a realistic response to the seismic pressures of social change and to the needs and aspirations of the people for whose life, liberty, and happiness governments are instituted among men.

ABOUT THE AUTHOR

Dr. Peter H. Odegard has had a distinguished career as a teacher, scholar, author, and adviser to foundations and governmental departments and commissions.

A graduate of the University of Washington, he earned his Doctor of Philosophy degree at Columbia University.

He was president of Reed College from 1945 to 1948 and taught at Columbia University, Williams College, Ohio State University, Amherst, Stanford University, Boston College, and the University of Pittsburgh.

During World War II he served first as a consultant and later as Assistant to the Secretary of the Treasury, for whom he wrote the basic policy and plan of organization for the War Finance Program.

For twelve years he was a member of the Phi Beta Kappa Senate.

He served as a consultant to the Ford Foundation and the Atomic Energy Commission and was a member of President Truman's Commission on Farm Labor.

He is the author of *Pressure Politics: The Story of the Anti-Saloon League, The American Public Mind, American Politics: A Study in Political Dynamics, Democracy in Transition, Religious Politics, The American Republic: Its Government and Politics,* and *The Power to Govern.*

At present Professor of Political Science at the University of California at Berkeley, he is working on a book to be called *Bonds of Freedom.*

This book has been set in Caledonia with display type of Consort. It was printed by letterpress on Mead's 60# Publishers' Imperial Text and bound in Curtis Tweedweave. The designer was Cynthia Muser, and the manufacturer was H. Wolff Book Manufacturing Co., Inc., New York.